ISLAM & ITS FOUNDER

ISLAM & ITS FOUNDER

(NON-CHRISTIAN RELIGIOUS SYSTEMS)

J. W. H. STOBART, B. A.

GYAN

Published by

GYAN

Gyan Publishing House
5, Ansari Road
Daryaganj, New Delhi-110002
Phone: 011-47034999, 9811692060
E-mail: books@gyanbooks.com

Distribution Network
gyanbooks.com
India, USA, Canada, UK, Australia, France

ISBN: 978-81-212-8650-3 (PB)
First Published, 1895

2nd Impression 2023

Printed at: Gyan Press, Delhi.

ISLAM & ITS FOUNDER
Author: J. W. H. STOBART

A MAP to illustrate ISLAMISM

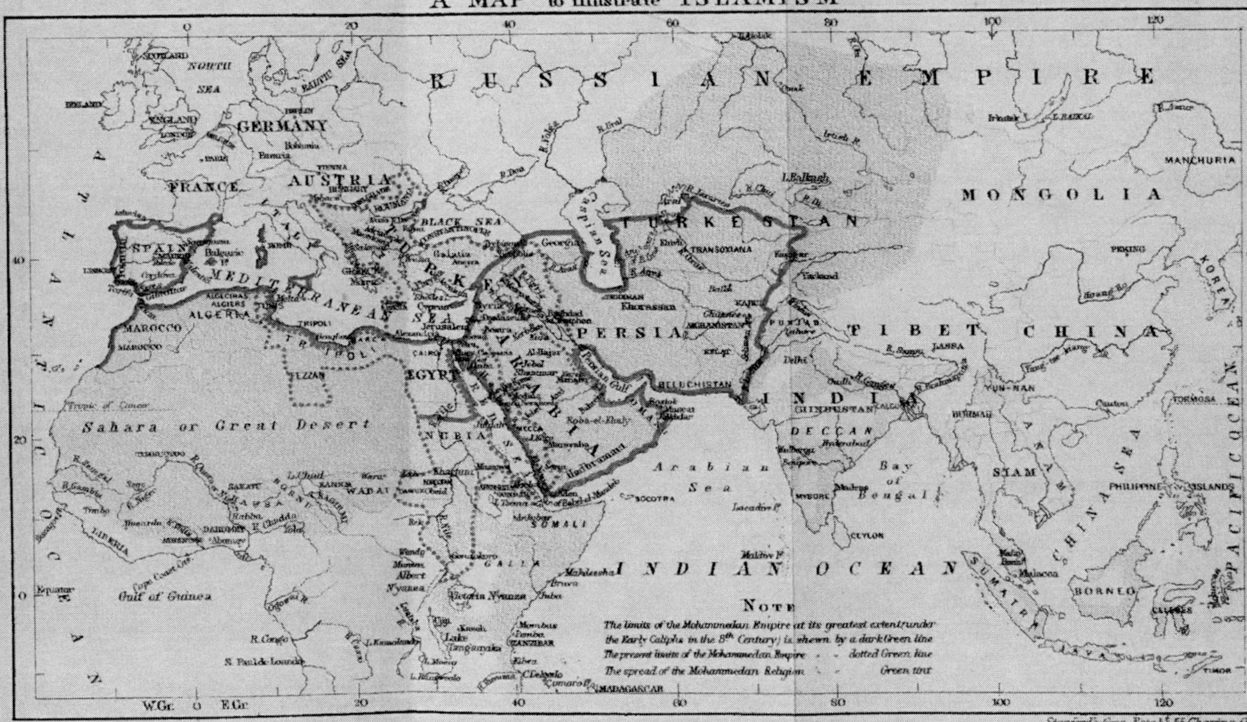

Stanford's Geog. Estabt. 55, Charing Cross.

London, Published by the Society for Promoting Christian Knowledge.

ISLAM & ITS FOUNDER.

BY

J. W. H. STOBART, B.A.,

PRINCIPAL, LA MARTINIERE COLLEGE, LUCKNOW.

WITH MAP.

PUBLISHED UNDER THE DIRECTION OF
THE COMMITTEE OF GENERAL LITERATURE AND EDUCATION
APPOINTED BY THE SOCIRTY FOR PROMOTING
CHRISTIAN KNOWLEDGE.

Nin:h Thousand.

SOCIETY FOR PROMOTING CHRISTIAN KNOWLEDGE
LONDON: NORTHUMBERLAND AVENUE, W.C.;
43, QUEEN VICTORIA STREET, E.C.
NEW YORK: E. & J. B. YOUNG & CO.
1895.

PREFACE.

I AM so much indebted to the researches of others for the contents of this little Manual, that I scarcely know where to begin my acknowledgments. My especial thanks are due to Sir W. Muir, for the valuable aid of his work [1]—confessedly the best on the subject,—which I have taken as my guide in these pages. Sale's translation is used in the quotations from the Koran, and from his "Preliminary Discourse" and "Notes" I have freely quoted. I have also found valuable aid in the writings of Freeman (*The Saracens*), Forster (*Geography of Arabia*), Kasimirski (*Koran*), Irving (*Life of Mahomet*), Monier Williams (*Indian Wisdom*), Lane (*Modern Egyptians, &c.*), Burton (*El Mecca and El Medineh*), Kennedy, the Rev. J. (*Christianity and the Religions of India*), Hughes, the Rev. T. P. (*Notes on Muhammadanism*), Lamartine, Prideaux, Deutsch, Bosworth Smith, Gibbon, and others who have written on the subject.

[1] "Life of Mahomet," 4 vols. 4to. London.

I have thought best to retain the spelling "Mahomet," "Koran," "Caliph," "Wahabee," &c., as being naturalized in our language, and as likely to hold their place till some uniform system of transliteration is generally adopted.[1]

With regard to the contents of this book, I am not conscious that any important matter connected with Islam, or regarding its founder, has been omitted. In treating of the leading features of the Mahometan system I have sought to state facts and results, rather than to attribute motives; and, whilst compromising nothing of the truth, have endeavoured to avoid everything which would appear like partisanship or prejudice.

Sincerely trusting that I may not, in any particular, have neglected the golden rule of Christian Charity in speaking of "the great antagonistic Creed," and fully conscious of the imperfections of my work, whose aim is to be a popular exposition of the subject, I now submit it to the indulgent criticism of the reader.

J. W. H. S.

CLIFTON, 5*th July*, 1876.

[1] We meet with "Muhammad," "Mohammed," "Mohammad"; Quran, Coran, Al-coran, C-kooran, &c. The verse-numbers are those of Kasimirski.

TABLE OF CONTENTS.

ISLAM AND ITS FOUNDER.

CHAPTER I.

GEOGRAPHY, EARLY HISTORY, AND PEOPLING OF ARABIA.

"JEZERET-UL-ARAB," or the Chersonese of Arabia, is the name given by its inhabitants to the great peninsula which, bordered by the Red Sea, the Indian Ocean, the Persian Gulf, and the deserts which extend to the Euphrates, stretches, in round numbers, from the 12th to the 34th degree of north latitude. Its length, from the Mediterranean to the Straits of Bab-el-Mandeb, is about 1,400 miles, its breadth across the neck of the peninsula is 800 miles, whilst its coast-line on the Indian Ocean approaches 1,200 miles. "Although Arabia is not greatly inferior in extent to India, it does not possess a single navigable river."[1] Few of its streams reach the ocean. Most of them exist only when swelled by the periodic rains, and, as a rule, lose themselves in the sandy plains. Arabia forms a part of that barren and nearly rainless region, of which the Sahara, in Africa, and the deserts of Shamo, in Thibet, form the eastern

[1] Muir, I. cxlvi.

and western boundaries. It embraces, within its extent, strange varieties of scenery and soil,—barren hills, vast sandy deserts uninhabited and uninhabitable, a rock-bound coast, stretches of excellent pasturage and fertile wadies, which, contrasted with the bleak wilderness around, charm the traveller with an unspeakable freshness and verdure.

The name Arabia was often used by old writers in a wide sense. Thus it is applied by Pliny to part of Mesopotamia; by Herodotus (ii. 12) to Syria, and to the coast of the Red Sea between it and the Nile valley. The general division of Arabia, by Greek and Roman writers, is into Arabia Deserta and Arabia Felix. This latter epithet is probably only a mistaken translation of "El Yemen,"—the land on the right hand, that is, of the south, for the Orientals faced east; as contrasted with Syria, which in Arabic is called "El Sham," or the country to the left of Mecca. The third division, Arabia Petraea, that is, Arabia of Petra, first appears in Ptolemy, applied to the Sinai district. Arabia Deserta was inhabited entirely by nomad tribes—Scenitæ—tent-men, and Saraceni. Arabia Felix was occupied by more settled tribes, as the Sabæi, &c. Their principal port was Aden, the Arabiæ Emporium of Ptolemy. The Arabians were never subdued, properly speaking, as a nation. Indeed, their innumerable tribal and political divisions, and the nature of the country, rendered their subjugation to a foreign power next to impossible. They gave to the Great King, as allies, not as subjects, a gift of one thousand talents of frankincense (Herodotus, iii. 97).

The Emperor Augustus (B.C. 24) sent an expedition of Arabian discovery and conquest, under Ælius Gallus, the Roman governor of Egypt; of which Pliny and Strabo have left accounts. The latter was a personal friend of the commander, and his narration may probably be relied upon. Great difference of opinion exists as to the geographical interpretation of the accounts extant. The expedition embarked from Cleopatris, the modern Suez, and, after a voyage of fifteen days, landed at "Leuke Kome," a port of the Hejaz, on the Arabian shore of the Red Sea. Partly owing to sickness, which delayed the army a year, and the treachery of the Arabian (Nabathean) King of Petra—Obodas, and his minister Syllæus, who for six months led the force alternately through deserts and fertile tracts, the expedition failed. Among other places which were taken and destroyed was Mariaba—a city six miles in circumference. Thence they proceeded to Marsyaba, the siege of which, from the strength of its fortifications and the scarcity of water, they were obliged to raise. They retreated, and in two months reached "Nera Kome," whence they embarked and landed at Myos Hormus, in Egypt. Mr. Forster[1] has sought, with apparent success, to identify these places; but Sir W. Muir thinks it "impossible to

[1] Vol. ii. sec. 6: "Leuke Kome"=El Haûra, or Horan, north of Yembo. "Nera Kome"=Yembo of the Calingii, or Beni Khaled. "Mariaba," identified with Mareb in Bahrein, on the Persian Gulf; not Mareb, the capital of the Sabeans, in Yemen. "Marsyaba"=Sabbia, or Sabe, north of Jebel, Climax Mons, in Wadi Najran.

recognize any of the towns through which the expedition passed."[1]

The Emperor Trajan (A.D. 105) made Arabia. from Damascus (El Sham) to the Red Sea, including the kingdom of Nabathea, a province under the governor of Syria, Cornelius Palma. Petra was its chief town; but it gradually sank with the loss of its caravan trade, and Bostra grew into importance. In the third century it was divided into two provinces, with these two towns as their respective capitals.

South Arabia (Yemen) has, from time to time, felt the influence of political vicissitude and foreign subjection, to which allusion will hereafter be made; but, generally speaking, Arabia, protected by the deserts of sand and sea which surround it, has but partially, and that only on its border lands, been subjected to those political revolutions which have affected the neighbouring countries; and its peoples present the picture of a race still, after centuries, retaining nationally the characteristics of their primitive condition, unchanged by successive deluges of alien immigration or foreign conquest.

A nearly continuous range of lofty hills and mountains runs down the peninsula, irregularly parallel to the Red Sea. In some places the hills approach the coast, whilst here and there they recede, so as to leave a broad margin of low land. From this longitudinal chain, three other ranges extend. In the north the Jebel Shammar, running eastward from about the head of the Gulf of Akaba; in the centre Jebel Ared,

[1] I. cxxii.

extending from near Mecca to the Persian Gulf; in the south irregular ranges of generally barren mountains overlooking the sea, extend from the Straits of Bab-el-Mandeb through the provinces of Hadhramaut and Oman.

Between the ranges of Jebel Shammar and Jebel Ared lies the high central land of Najd. It is a lofty plateau or steppe, rising to the height of some 9,000 feet, its water-shed generally being from west to east. It is a fertile country, and produces the finest breed of horses in Arabia.

The Hejaz, lying between Najd and the Red Sea, and running along the latter, includes the sacred cities of Mecca and Medina, with their respective ports of Jiddah and Yembo. It is about 100 miles broad, the land generally rising to the granite peaks of Jebel Kora, whence eastward is the high land of Najd. It is the holy land of Islam. It was conquered by Muhammad Ali, of Egypt, and in 1840 incorporated with the empire of Turkey.

The south-western portion of the peninsula is the fertile Yemen, where perennial streams flow from the mountains to the sea. It is rich in corn-fields and coffee-gardens, and its soil and vegetation entitle it to the name it bears of "Arabia Felix." North of Yemen lies the district of Najran. Politically, Yemen is under the government of an Imam who resides at Sanâ: its chief port is Mocha.

Hadhramaut lies along the south coast, which, though presenting from the sea a nearly uniform appearance of barrenness and desolation, is a short distance inland fruitful in the highest degree. A glowing description of it is to be found in Wellsted's "Travels in Arabia" (vol. i. pp. 115, 116). He says that the country about Minna, in the Jebel-el-Akhdar, or green mountains of Oman, abounds in the most luxuriant cultivation. Verdant fields of grain stretch for miles; streams of water flowing in every direction, groves of citron, almond, and orange trees, and a happy, contented peasantry, make up a picture worthy of Araby the blest.

The chief towns of Oman are Rostok and Muscat. The Imam of the latter town exercises sway in Oman, and as far into the interior as he can make his influence felt. South of Yamama lies the great dessert of Akhaf, which extends from near Mecca to Oman. On its border-lands the neighbouring tribes find, after the periodic rains, pasturage for their flocks and herds. Some of its arid tracts are reported never to have been explored. It is called by the Bedouins "Roba-el-Khaly," the empty abode. The only habitable spot in its dreary expanse of sand is Wadi-Jebryn, by which place the Arabs of Najd travel in winter to Hadhramaut. Along the Persian Gulf lies the province of Bahrein.

Arabia is a land of drought and barrenness. Some of its desert sandy wastes and granite hills are refreshed by scarcely a single shower in the year; at other times violent rains rapidly fill the tanks and wadies, and give rise to a luxuriant and intermittent vegetation. The date-palm is almost the only tree, and the weary traveller, as he traverses the country, finds but scanty shelter from the glaring sun. Aromatic herbs and a coarse undergrowth take the place of our grassy fields, and afford excellent pasturage to vast flocks, and to a noble breed of horses. In the higher lands, where well watered, a greater luxuriance prevails. Coffee, dates, and other fruits, cotton, balsam, myrrh, and frankincense are, together with "dhurra," which takes the place of corn, its staple products and exports. Arabia has no native industry, but is dependent on other countries for manufactured commodities. Its intellectual supremacy has long since departed; though schools exist throughout the country, little is taught beyond the reading of the Koran, a little elementary arithmetic, and science.

The mode of life of the Arabs is of three kinds: either they are nomadic (Bedouin), obtaining their livelihood from the rearing of camels, horses, cattle, and sheep, pitching their tents within certain limits, where water and pasturage are most abundant; or they are engaged in the transport of merchandise along the trading routes through the desert, in search of which employment they travel over the country with their camels; or they are sedentary, dwelling in towns either inland or on the seaboard, and engage in commerce with the interior or with the ports on the coast, on the opposite shores of Africa and Persia, or with India. In ancient times commercial intercourse was confined almost exclusively to the land, for in those days the trader trusted to the treacherous ocean as little as possible; and the spices and precious wares of Arabia and India were conveyed to the northern marts on the "ship of the desert" by settled routes, the halting-places being fixed at regular intervals, where shade, water, and provender were to be obtained. Here the weary traveller and his more wearied beasts of burden could rest and refresh themselves. At some of these halting-places regular towns in time arose, supported by the traffic which in many cases had called them into existence.

There appear to have been two chief routes, one from Yemen through the Hejaz, passing Mecca and Petra, chiefly supplying Egypt and Palestine; and another from Hadhramaut by the Persian Gulf, and thence branching off to the Euphrates valley, and chief towns of Syria,—Damascus and Tyre.

The prophet Ezekiel (B.C. 600), c. xxvii., in taking up the lamentation of Tyrus, speaks of its traffic with Arabia, the multitude of its wares (v. 16), its spices and gold (v. 22), and mentions some of the ports of Yemen and Hadhramaut, Haran, and Canneh and Eden, which retain their names to this day.

The western caravan route was in use in Mahomet's time, and his great-grandfather Hashim died at Gaza when on a mercantile expedition to Syria. Eventually the growing skill in navigation during Roman times annihilated the caravan trade, and substituted the sea route. The holy city of Mecca felt the loss of this inland traffic, but in its shrine—the Kaaba,—universally recognized as a place of pilgrimage throughout the peninsula, it possessed an element of life unknown at Petra; and with the rise and progress of Islam continued to flourish, and still thrives on the stream of pilgrims who visit it.

Living thus in tents, or in temporary dwellings,

and leading a free, wandering life, the Arab is simple and temperate in his habits and wants. He is generous and reverential in his mode of thought, acute and imaginative, delighting in eloquence, and easily touched by the charms of poetry. He is sudden and quick in honour, addicted to revenge as a sacred duty, yet strongly bound by the laws of hospitality. His character has its dark side too. He is careless of human life, and considers every stranger who is not of his kindred or tribe, or an ally, an enemy, whom, if occasion require, he will not scruple to circumvent by the blackest treachery. He is, as a rule, bigoted and selfish, and prone to debauchery; his reverence degenerates into fanaticism, and he is regardless of suffering in others. Cleanliness and the ordinary laws of sanitation are ignored. Burckhardt draws a deplorable picture of the filthy state of Mecca during his visit.

The remote ancestry of the Arab race has been represented as involved in much obscurity. Historians and geographers, in seeking to fix it with any degree of accuracy, have as their guides the following sources of information:—

(1) The Scripture record in the Old Testament.

(2) The records of Greek and Roman writers.

(3) The present names of places, regions, and tribes.

(4) Information regarding the local habits and characteristics supplied by modern travellers.

(5) Arab traditions, and the writings of their own historians.

Of the above, the Scripture records are the

only sure guides in any attempt to penetrate the darkness of their early history. From classical sources information of high value is also to be derived, and the names of places, regions, and nations, either obsolete or still remaining, form data of very great authority in this field of investigation. Tradition has, especially with such a nation, its value; but the Arab genealogies and their own accounts of their early ancestry are so mixed up with fabulous details, their chronology is so evidently manufactured, contradictory and foolish, as to merit little credence.

From such authorities the industry of modern research seems to have set in clear light the ancestry of this ancient people, and demonstrated the strict and literal accuracy, regarding the post-diluvian peopling of the world, of the Mosaic records, and of the other scattered notices to be found throughout the books of the Old Testament.[1]

Any information derived from ethnological or geographical sources which illustrates and confirms the Mosaic record cannot fail to be of the highest value to the Christian reader; and an intimate knowledge of Arabia in its past and present state, its traditions and tribal occupations and local nomenclature, its monuments and antiquities, will be found satisfactorily to sustain the sacred account of the distribution of mankind after the Flood, and has paramount claims on the Christian scholar and theologian.

For however firm our belief in the authenticity

[1] On this subject the reader should consult "The Geography of Arabia," by the Rev. Mr. Forster.

of the books of the Old Testament as the only sure and authentic guide in the study of the early history of our race, still, when we find living memorials and undesigned confirmations of the same in Arabia, we cannot but receive the same with feelings of grateful recognition. From the authorities mentioned above, it may be shown that the Arab race is sprung from the five great patriarchal stocks of (1) Cush, (2) Shem, (3) Ishmael, (4) Keturah, and (5) Esau.

The limits of this work and its especial object induce me, reluctantly, to abandon the attempt to give the reader any detailed account of the settlements in Arabia of the children of Cush and Shem, of Esau and Keturah. The Old Testament records, by incidental allusions, afford the most literal proofs of their migration thither.[1] Of Cushite settlements the clearest traces are still to be found on the coast of the Persian Gulf, and in the province of Oman. In the word Chuzestan, or the land of Cush; in the names Asabi or Sabi (Seba), the Hammæum Littus of Pliny (Ham), the island of Aval (Havilah), the chief of the Bahrein group, and in Regma (Raamah), and Dadena (Dedan), probable memorials of the ancient Scripture names still remain.[2] Sale, in his "Preliminary Discourse," says, "Others of the Arabs were the posterity of Ham by his son Cush, which name is in the Scripture constantly given to the Arabs and their country, though our version renders it Ethiopia; but,

[1] Conf. Num. xii. 1 (margin); Ezek. xxviii. 20-22; Ps. lxxii. 10; Job i. 15; Habak. iii. 7; iv. 39-41.

[2] Conf. Gen. x. 6-8; Forster, i. 73; Muir, I. cx.

strictly speaking, the Cushites[1] did not inhabit Arabia, properly so called, but the banks of the Euphrates and the Persian Gulf, whither they came from Chuzestan, or Susiana, the original settlement of their father" (p. 9).

Very ancient tradition pronounces the great existing race of the Beni Kahtan to be the descendants of Shem, the stock of the patriarch Eber by his second son Joktan.[2] This cherished tradition of the Arab race, which claims the patriarch Joktan (or Kahtan) as the ancestor of the race (which has spread from near Mecca in the Hejaz, throughout the whole of Yemen and the south coast of Oman, and is found also in the Najd, having dominated over all other races in those parts), is supported by strong evidence in the names of places and localities still existing. It may be clearly shown that the very names given in the Old Testament are to be identified in the settlement of the great Semitic race, and thus that here again the sacred record, Arab tradition, the statements of the classical writers, and modern geography are unanimous in their independent testimony.

The descendants of Abraham by Keturah, and of Esau,[3] gained a strong and permanent footing in the northern parts of the peninsula and on the shores

[1] On the identity of the name "Midianite" and "Cushite" see Forster, vol. i. p. 12, *et seq.*

[2] Conf. D'Herbelot, art. "Arab," i. p. 345; W. Irving, "Life of Mahomet," p. 112; Forster, i. 77–175; Muir, "The Life of Mahomet," 1. p. cvii(x).; Lamartine, "Hist. de T," i. p. 370; Sale, P. D., p. 1.

[3] Gen. xxv. 1–6; xxxvi. 1–43.

of the Gulf of Akaba; and frequent reference to them as peoples of Arabia is to be found in the prophetic books of the Old Testament.[1] The greatness of the race of Esau, as foretold in Scripture, was abundantly fulfilled in after-times. It is allowed by the best authorities[2] that the great Arab nation of Amalek was descended from the grandson of Esau; and the richness and fertility of their possessions is referred to by a recent traveller.[3] The name of this race is still imprinted on the shores of the Red Sea, in "Ras Edom" and "Jezeret Edom," a cape and island of the Hejaz. The existence of the Edomite settlements found there, in Yemen, and on the Persian Gulf, supports the statement of the classical writers that the Edomites are identical with the ancient Idumeans, who commanded the navigation of the Erythrean Sea, and renders the suggestion probable that the name of this great commercial nation was once imposed upon the waters of the Indian Ocean.[4]

As the reputed ancestor of the prophet of Mecca the descendants of Ishmael deserve particular notice.[5] Few can read without emotion the story of the expulsion of Hagar and her son Ishmael (born B.C. 1910); how they wandered in the wilderness of Beersheba solitary and in exile; how,

[1] Isaiah, xxi. 13.

[2] Muir, I. cxiii., notes.

[3] Robinson, "Bib. Res.," ii. 551, 552.

[4] "When the Adites sent messengers to the Kaaba to implore for rain, Mecca was in the hands of the tribe of Amalek" (Sale's "Koran," p. 124).

[5] Conf. Forster, i. 176–316.

when the water in her bottle was spent, she cast the child under one of the shrubs of the desert, lest she should see him die; and yet, how, from this the depth of her anguish, God's providence was fulfilled, how her eyes were opened, and she saw the well of water; and how that son, for whom the aged Patriarch had besought the Almighty (before the birth of the chosen seed) "that he might dwell before Him," was blessed exceedingly, and became a great nation, his children being, "by their towns and by their castles, twelve princes according to their nations" (Gen. xvii. 18–20, and xxv. 12–18).

In the book of Genesis the names of Ishmael's sons are given, and the bounds of their habitation; for we are told that he lived "in the wilderness of Paran," and that they dwelt "from Havilah unto Shur, that is before Egypt" (Gen. xxv. 18). Abandoned and almost repudiated by his father, and coming as a stranger with his mother to these regions, it can easily be imagined that to Hagar alone would reference be made concerning the ancestral stock, and this is abundantly found to be the case.

Constant reference is made in Holy Scripture to the Hagarites and the Hagarenes, and they are represented as inhabiting those very parts of northern Arabia, towards which Hagar was sent. Thus, in Psalm lxxxiii. we read of "the tabernacles of Edom and the Ishmaelites, of Moab and the Hagarenes," nations dwelling in close proximity, in the lands spreading southwards from the Holy Land towards the Red Sea. In the days of Saul (B.C. 1095–1055), the sons of Reuben, a pastoral tribe whose settlements lay to the south-east of the Dead Sea, "made war with the Hagarites, and dwelt in their tents throughout all the east land of Gilead" (1 Chron. v. 10); and again in the days of Jeroboam (B.C. 975-954), the tribes which dwelt beyond Jordan "made war with the Hagarites, with Jetur, and Nephish, and Nodab," where we again have mention of the maternal name (Hagar) in conjunction with those of the youngest sons of Ishmael (1 Chron. v. 18, 19, and Gen. xxv. 15).

The synonymous use of the terms "Midianites" and "Ishmaelites" serves to fix the situation of the country inhabited by the latter (Gen. xxxvii. 28); and St. Paul, in speaking of the old and new covenants, expressly states that Mount Sinai, "which gendereth to bondage, which is Agar. For this Agar is Mount Sinai in Arabia" (Gal. iv. 24, 25).

In the books of the Old Testament frequent mention is made of Nebajoth (or Nebaioth) and Kedar, the eldest, two sons of Ishmael. Thus Isaiah (lx. 6, 7), in speaking of the glories of the Redeemer's reign, says "that they from Sheba shall bring gold and incense . . . . . all the flocks of Kedar . . . . . and the rams of Nebaioth shall minister unto thee," a declaration coupling these two names together, and pointing to their pastoral occupation; whilst the Psalmist's allusion to the "tents of Kedar" (Ps. cxx. 5, 7) intimates clearly the nomadic mode of life which they led.

The "wilderness of Paran" is recovered, on the authority of Ptolemy, in "Pharan Oppidum" and "Pharan Promontorium," which latter terminates the Peninsula of Sinai; and in the "Pharanitæ," described by him as extending northward from the head of the Gulf of Akaba to the desert of Tyh. The whole province of Bahrein, which once bore the Cushite name of Havilah, is now known among the Arab tribes inhabiting it chiefly and properly by the Ishmaelite name of Hagar. The latter name occurs in Yemen, showing probably that offshoots of the race migrated thither. Josephus (who flourished in the first century after Christ) affirms the existence of twelve Arab nations sprung from the sons of Ishmael; and St. Jerome also says "that Kedar is a country of the Saracens, who in Scripture are called Ishmaelites." [1]

The descendants of the eldest son of Ishmael are to be identified with the "Nabatheans" of the classical writers, described as the most illustrious kingdom and people of Arabia. They are the Beni Nabat of the Mahometan writers. Petra [2] was the capital of their kingdom, which from it took the name of "Arabia Petraea," and was comprised within the limits of the ancient Edom. The strength of the sons of

[1] Forster, i. p. 200. Niebuhr, iii. 293.

[2] Pliny says of Petra that "the Nabatæi inhabit a city called Petra, in a hollow somewhat less than two miles in circumference, surrounded by inaccessible mountains . . . . distant from the town of Gaza on the coast 600 miles." Strabo writes that it is fortified with a barrier of rocks, has excellent springs of water, and that outside the city the country is a desert. To Burckhardt belongs the honour of being the first to penetrate to this long-lost city. Dressed as an Arab Sheikh, he passed the mountains of Edom, and on the 22nd August, 1812, entered Petra by the wonderful gorge of Sik. He describes the town as surrounded with vineyards and fruit-trees, the grapes being especially fine ("Alps of Arabia," pp. 201–204).

Nebajoth was well illustrated, and perhaps explained by that of their capital, which, situated in the midst of deserts, and, itself a natural fortress, became the high road of the commerce between Yemen and Syria, the Persian Gulf, and the ports and marts of Egypt.

Three centuries before the Christian era, we hear of them baffling the attacks of the Macedonian monarchs of Babylon behind the rocky ramparts of Petra. Their kingdom extended from Egypt to Palestine, and down the shores of the Red Sea. In the reign of Augustus we have seen that their king Obodas assisted Ælius Gallus in his unsuccessful expedition against Yemen. At the beginning of the Christian era they gradually became dependent on Rome, and their kingdom was annexed (A.D. 105) by the emperor Trajan.

The Old Testament evidences for the existence of Kedar, as a powerful people of Arabia, are full and explicit;[1] and on a reference to these it will be found that their details are compatible with the settlements of Kedar being in the Hejaz, near or between Mecca and Medina; and it is on this very ground that Pliny places a people of similar name, identical with the Kedarys, or Beni Kedar.

The tradition of the Arabs themselves represents Kedar to have settled in the Hejaz, and from this patriarch the family of the Coreish, the guardians of the Kaaba, always boasted their descent.[2] Though

[1] Isaiah xxi. 11, 17; xlii. 10–12; lx. 7; Jer. ii. 10, 11.

[2] *Vide* Forster, i. p. 251, on this point. Muir (Life of Mahomet, 1. p. ccix.) gives a quotation from M. C. de Percival (vol. i. p. 183):—"The Arabs of the Hejaz and Najd have al-

traces of the remaining sons of Ishmael are to be found, it may generally be said "that they either mingled with the other tribes, or, penetrating the peninsula (south), have escaped observation."[1]

In addition to the immigrants whom we have now considered, and who, as a "mingled people" (Jer. xxv. 24), formed the permanent inhabitants of Arabia, there were in later times large colonies and tribes of Jews scattered throughout the peninsula. They are found holding lands and castles, and occupying important positions in the country, especially about Medina, in which and in its vicinity numerous powerful tribes of them were settled. Kheibar was one of their strongholds. In the eighth year of the Hejira the Jews of this place were attacked by Mahomet, their lands and fortresses fell into his hands, and their chief, Kinana, tortured to death. Many of their numbers perished, and those who remained were exterminated in the caliphate of Omar. Two of Mahomet's wives were of this religion, Safia, widow of the murdered Kinana, and Rihana.

A force of 500 Jews formed part of the contingent supplied by the Nabathean king to Ælius Gallus in his expedition. One of the kings of the Himyarite dynasty in Yemen, named Dzu-Nowas (A.D. 490 to 525), having on a visit to Medina (Yathrib),

ways (?) regarded Ishmael as their ancestor. This conviction—the source of their respect for the memory of Abraham—is too general, too deep not to repose on a real foundation. In fine, Mahomet, who gloried in his Ishmaelitish origin, was never contradicted on that point by his enemies the Jews."

[1] Muir, I, cxii.

of which half the population were Jews, embraced their creed, invaded Najran, for the purpose of extirpating the Christian faith, which had made very considerable progress in that province. His cruelties, especially in having thrown the Christian martyrs into a trench filled with burning materials, are alluded to in the Koran (sura lxxxv. 4 *et seq.*). The number of victims are stated at no less than 20,000 (Muir, I. clxii.). This persecution of the Christians of Yemen moved to vengeance the Prince of Abyssinia, who was of the Nestorian sect. An army was sent over the narrow gulf, and the expedition (A.D. 525) ended in the death of Dzu-Nowas, and the subjection of Yemen, which became a dependency of the Abyssinian king.

Aryat and Abraha were the successive viceroys. Vigorous missionary efforts were made to Christianize the country. A magnificent cathedral was built at Sanā, and it was hoped that the Arab tribes would be diverted from Mecca to the new shrine. These hopes were frustrated, and in revenge for his disappointment, and for certain indignities which had been practised in the cathedral itself, Abraha set out to destroy the Kaaba. The expedition (A.D. 570) failed, and its leader perished. The event, which took place in the year of Mahomet's birth, is recorded in the Koran, sura cv., entitled "The Elephant."

The destruction of Jerusalem by Titus (A.D. 70) probably scattered many Christians throughout Arabia, in nearly all quarters of which they would be likely to meet with sympathizers with their own faith.

The Christian religion had gradually and partially penetrated into Arabia, and gained scattered converts, though it never succeeded in taking a permanent hold there, or in superseding the existing idolatry. The opposition which it would meet with from the Jews must not be forgotten; and we must also remember how antagonistic the general habits of the Arab race would be to the spread of the gospel. "The haughty temper and revengeful code of the Arab tribes, and their licentious practices, were all alike hostile to the humble and forgiving precepts of Christian morality."[1]

Still, Christianity was not unrepresented in the peninsula. In the fourth century Petra was the residence of a Metropolitan, whose diocese embraced the ancient Idumæa and Nabathea; and several Christian bishoprics were established in Arabia subject to him. Abd-Kelal (A.D. 275), Himyarite king of Yemen, was a Christian. He is said to have been converted by a Christian stranger, who, in consequence of the king's defection, was murdered. This is the first intimation of Christianity in Yemen.[2] During the reign of Marthad (A.D. 330), son of Abd-Kelal, the emperor Constantius sent a Christian embassy to the court of the Himyarite monarch, who is called "Prince of the Sabæans and Homerites," and certain privileges were gained from the tolerant king for the professors of the Christian faith visiting or residing in Yemen. Three churches were built at Izafar the royal residence, at Aden, and on the Persian gulf. No important event followed this em-

[1] Muir, I. ccxxxvi. [2] Ib. I. clx.

bassy, but the knowledge is gained thereby that the inhabitants of Yemen at the time were partly Jewish and partly Pagan. The latter practised circumcision, and sacrificed to the sun and moon, and to other divinities.[1]

The cruelties of Dzu-Nowas, a subsequent king of Yemen, to the Christians have been spoken of above. Christian anchorites, dwelling in their solitary cells in Arabia Petræa, must have aided in spreading a knowledge of their belief. It reached the kingdom of Hira, a town near Kufa, on the Euphrates, and the seat of an important Arab dynasty; and, under Noman (319—418 A.D.), spread in his dominions; and there is good reason for believing that he himself had embraced the same faith. In the reign of Mundzir III. of Hira (513—562 A.D.) a Christian embassy of two bishops, sent by the Patriarch of Antioch, failed to gain over the king to their tenets, though he granted toleration to its followers throughout his territories. Noman V., of Hira, the last of the Lakhmite dynasty (A.D. 583—605), was a Christian. Many of the Arab tribes were Christians, and it was generally adopted in Najran about the close of the fourth century.[2]

The princes of Axum, in Abyssinia, a powerful and extensive state, were Christians of the Nestorian sect. The persecutions practised in turn by differing Christian sects contributed to scatter believers throughout the East, and drove numbers into Arabia. "Christianity was there known, living examples of it

[1] Muir, I. clx. Gibbon, "Decline and Fall," cap. xx.
[2] Muir, I. ccxxix.

were to be found amongst the native tribes; the New Testament was respected, if not reverenced, as a book that claimed to be divine, and some of its facts and doctrines were admitted without dispute."[1] Yet its progress was disabled and impeded by the differences of contending schisms, which had substituted "the puerilities of a debasing superstition for the pure and expansive faith of the early ages."[2] To this subject we shall hereafter return, when we come to consider the nature of the influence exercised by Jewish and Christian doctrine, practices, and innovations on the religion established by Mahomet. Enough has at present been said regarding the existence of the two religions in the Arabian peninsula. Such, then, is a general sketch of the elements which went to make up the great Arab race.

[1] Muir, I. cxxix. [2] Ib. I. ccxxvi.

GENEALOGICAL TABLE *of the Family of* COREISH, *and the Ancestors of* MAHOMET.

[Consult Sale, P. D., § i. p. 9; Muir, I. cxcv.; Prideaux, p. 1.]

No. I.

ABRAHAM [b. 1996, d. 1822 B.C.], the father by Hagar of ISHMAEL [b. 1910], married a daughter of Modadh, Jorhamite, chief of Mecca, and had children. From them descended ADNAN [b. B.C. 130], the father of MAADD; from whom, in the seventh generation, descended NADHR [b. A.D. 134], the father of Malik, the father of FIHR COREISH [b. A.D. 200]. The descendants of Fihr Coreish were as follows:—

- FIHR COREISH [b. A.D. 200].
  - GHALIB.
    - LOWAY.
      - CAAB.
        - MORRAH.
          - KILAB [b. A.D. 365].
            - CUSSAI [see Table No. II.]
              - ABD-AL-DAR.
              - ABD MENAF.
              - ABD-AL-OZZA. From whom descended Zobeir, Khadija, &c.
            - ZOHRA. From whom descended Wahb, the father of Amina, the mother of Mahomet.
          - TAYM. From whom came Abu Bekr, 1st Caliph.
          - YOKDAH. From whom Khalid, and Abu Jahl, &c.
        - ADA. From whom Omar ibn al Khattab, 2nd Caliph.

Family of HASHIM.

No. II.

- CASSIA.
  - ABD-AL-DAR.
    - ⋮ From whom descended Abd-al-Ozza, the father of Talha, who carried the standard at Ohod, A.D. 625, and was slain with his brothers and sons [*vide* Muir, iii. 166].
      - TALHA.
        - OTHMAN IBN TALHA. Continued with his descendants custody of the key of the Kaaba.—Muir, iv. 128.
  - ABD-MENAF [born A.D. 430.] {[The succession and ages of his sons doubtful.]
    - AL-MUTTALIB.
    - HASHIM (married Salma).
      - ABD-AL-MUTTALIB.
        - HARITH.
        - ZOBIER.
        - ABU TALIB.
          - ALI + (Fatima, daughter of Mahomet), 4th Caliph.
            - HASAN, 5th Caliph, resigned in favour of Muavia.
            - HOSEIN, killed at the Kerbela, A.H. 61.
            - ZAINAD (daughter).
            - MOHASAN. Died an infant.
          - JAFAR, killed at Muta, A.D. 629.
        - ABU LAHAB, married to Omm Jemil. Conf. Koran, chap. cxi.
        - ABDALLAH. + Amina.
          - MAHOMET, born A.D. 570, died A.D. 632.
        - ABBAS, custodian of the cup of Zem-Zem.—Muir, iv. 128.
        - HAMZA, killed at Ohod, 625,
    - ABD SHAMS.
    - NAUFAL.

CHAPTER II.

ANCIENT RELIGIOUS OBSERVANCES OF THE ARABS, AND ANCESTRY OF MAHOMET.

WE have the assurance that Noah was "a perfect man, and walked with God" (Gen. vii. 9), and as a "preacher of righteousness" (2 Peter ii. 5), having with his sons been witness of the Flood, handed down to his posterity the worship of the True God. This knowledge could not have been lost when the descendants of Shem wandered forth to subdue the fertile lands of the South, nor at the time when the Abrahamic stocks entered Arabia, for Noah was contemporary with the "Father of the Faithful," and Shem lived beyond the time when Ishmael and Keturah, with their sons, had left their original homes.

Yet we find that idolatry before this had crept in, and that Terah, the father of Abraham, had obscured the worship of "the Lord God of Shem," and "served other gods" (Joshua xxiv. 2); Laban (B.C. 1739) had images; and Amaziah (B.C. 820), after the slaughter of the Edomites, brought away "the gods of the children of Seir" (2 Chron. xxv. 14).

But idolatry,—that yearning of the heart for a

visible object of devotion, something that the eye can see and the hands handle, the worship of the creature more than the Creator,—the idolatry which sprang up among the kindred nation of Israel was from time to time checked by the divine interference peculiar to the theocracy under which the chosen people lived.[1]

Without these restraints, no wonder the less favoured descendants of Shem in Arabia rapidly degenerated into gross and universal idolatry. There is reason for believing that the worship of the heavenly bodies was the oldest form of their spiritual decadence ; and it is natural perhaps to expect that, living in such a country, their idolatry would take that form. Leading a nomad life, their existence was emphatically one spent in the open air ; by day amidst their flocks, and herds, and encampments, and by night habitually sleeping beneath their rainless heavens. Amid the silence of night, with the busy scenes of day over, and no change visible but that of the constellations rising and setting, or fading with the dawn, the Chaldean shepherd or the Arab chief, in the absence of a diviner revelation, came to consider that human events were influenced by these heavenly luminaries.

Seeing the changes brought about by the seasons, and observing the influence of the sun and moon on the earth ; noticing, too, that the products of

[1] Confer 2 Kings xxiii. 5–11, where we have recorded that Josiah (B.C. 641—610) put down "them that burnt incense to —the sun and to the moon and to the planets and all the host of heaven." Confer Joshua xxiv. 14, 15 ; Acts vii. 42, 43.

their fields and vineyards and the periodic rains corresponded with the heliacal rising of certain constellations, they naturally supposed that these phenomena had influence [1] over the destiny of individuals and nations. Thus astrology, or the art of divining by the position of the stars, became one of the oldest superstitions of the human race.

The early religion of the Arabs, then, was a kind of Sabeanism, and "chiefly consisted in worshipping the fixed stars and planets and the angels and their images, which they honoured as inferior deities, and whose intercession they begged as their mediators with God." [2] This worship of the heavenly bodies is alluded to in the book of Job (xxxviii. 31—33), and the names of certain constellations which were adored are given. Sacrifices to the sun, &c., we learn, took place in Yemen even as late as the fourth century. Herodotus (iii. 8) writes of the Arabs that "they acknowledge no other gods but Bacchus and Urania . . . they call Bacchus Orotal, and Urania Alilat." [3] He also states that in giving pledges the hands of the contracting persons were cut, and while invoking their deities the blood was smeared on seven stones placed between them. The invocation of Urania, identical, doubtless, with

[1] The tendency to worship the host of heaven is anticipated in Scripture. Confer Deut. iv. 19, and xvii. 3; 2 Kings xvii. 16, and xxi. 3; Jerem. xviii. 13.

[2] Sale, P. D., p. 15.

[3] The people of Tayif, near Mecca, had an idol of their own, called Lât, which they honoured as the Meccans did that at the Kaaba. They were jealous of the superior fame of the Meccan shrine.

the Meccan idol Allât and the mystic number seven, connects their worship with that of the seven heavenly bodies, having real or apparent motion, known to them. The seven circuits of the devout pilgrim round the chief shrine, the Kaaba, are thought to be emblematical of the revolutions of the heavenly bodies.

The worship of rude unshapen stones may have arisen from the practice of carrying away to distant parts stones from the sacred inclosure at Mecca, and of paying to them the ceremonial observances usual at the Kaaba. It is easy to understand how in time the original motive would be forgotten, and the idols remain to increase and perpetuate idolatry. Five gods of the antediluvian world are mentioned in the Koran (sura lxxi. 22, 23), and these having been recovered after the Deluge (?) were worshipped by certain tribes under various forms. Each tribe had its special divinity, and each family its idol penates, which were saluted on leaving and returning home. The worship of the sun at Saba is mentioned by Mahomet (Koran, xxvii. 24): "Of angels or intelligences which they worshipped the Koran makes mention of three only, Allat, Alozza, and Manah, who are called the daughters of God."[1]

The heavenly bodies especially worshipped were Canopus (Sohail), Sirius (Alshira),[2] Aldebaran in Taurus, with the planets Mercury (Otarod), Venus (Al Zohirah), Jupiter (Al Moshtari); and Sale states that the temple at Mecca was said to have been

[1] Sale, P. D., p. 17; Koran, sura liii. 19, 20.

[2] Koran, sura liii. 50.

consecrated to Saturn (Zohal). About the Kaaba was the famous idol Hobal, the tutelary deity of Mecca, supposed to have the power of granting rain, surrounded by 360 others of smaller size, representing the saints and divinities, which could be invoked on each day of the year.[1] Of the form of the adoration paid to these idols little is known, but by analogy it may be assumed that the occasions of their pilgrimage would be connected with their domestic or family history, and chiefly the absorbing desire for offspring. There is a record of an embassy sent to the Kaaba to implore for rain in a time of drought.[2] Solemn engagements were ratified before the celebrated "Black Stone."[3]

Though there are authentic accounts of idolatrous shrines and places of pilgrimage in Yemen, and as far as Hira, yet the most famous throughout the entire peninsula was the Kaaba. Arab tradition has surrounded this shrine with a cloud of legendary story, and attributed its first building to Adam and Eve, who after their expulsion from Paradise and devious

[1] D'Herbelot, *voc.* Hobal.

[2] Kasimirski, "Le Koran," p. 350. Lokman.

[3] Muir, ii. 49. "It is the characteristic of the Oriental, and especially of the Semitic mind, to see in every event, even the most trivial, a direct supernatural interference, wrought by the innumerable unseen ministers, both good and evil, of the Divine will. The definite form in which the belief clothed itself was, by the admission of the Jews themselves, derived from Babylon. Even the most ordinary forces of nature and passions of the mind were by them regarded as angels. The Jews would have interpreted quite literally the verse Ps. civ. 4." (Farrar, "Life of Christ," ii. p. 465, Excursus vii.)

wanderings, met at length in penitence and forgiveness near Mecca, and were allowed to build a temple in imitation of that in which they had offered their pure worship in the garden of Eden![1] Destroyed by the Flood, an angel revealed its site to the forlorn Hagar and Ishmael perishing with thirst in the desert, and there, to their needs bubbled forth the waters of the well Zem Zem.[2] The fountain attracts a neighbouring tribe of Amalekites, who build near its waters the town of Mecca, and with them the youthful Ishmael and his mother find protection and rest.[3]

Here Ishmael was visited by his father Abraham, who, in obedience to Divine command, is about to offer him up on a neighbouring hill, but some vicarious sacrifice is accepted, and they set about the work of rebuilding the Kaaba on its

[1] On their expulsion from Paradise, so the story goes, Adam fell in Serendib, or Ceylon, where the footprint on the top of Adam's Peak (attributed by his priests to Buddha) was, say the Mahometans, made by our first parent. Eve fell in Arabia, near Jiddah, and after two hundred years' separation they were permitted to come together on Mount Arafat, near Mecca, where they lived many years. The tomb of Eve is shown near Jiddah, outside the walls. It is sixty cubits long and twelve wide, for Adam and Eve in stature equalled the tallest palm-tree! Adam's place of interment is variously stated to be near Mecca and in Ceylon. Cf. D'Herbelot, art. "Adam"; Koran, sura ii. 34, 35; Sale's note *ad loc.*

[2] The Mahometans say that "Zem Zem and Siloah are the two fountains of Paradise" (Farrar, "Life of Christ," ii. p. 81).

[3] The settlement of Hagar and Ishmael at Mecca is alluded to in the Koran, thus: "O Lord, I [Abraham] have caused some of my offspring to settle in an unfruitful valley, near thy holy house, O Lord, that they be constant at prayer" (Sura xiv. 40).

ancient site.[1] To assist in this work, the angel Gabriel brought them one of the stones of Paradise —the celebrated Black Stone—which rose and fell as the divinely-aided masons progressed with the work. This "Heavenly Stone" was, on completion of the work, inserted in an outer corner of the wall of the Kaaba, and after varying fortunes is still devoutly kissed or touched on each of the seven circuits round the Temple. At first it was bright and translucent, but its present colour is supposed to reflect, but too truly, the salutations of sinful mortals.[2]

Grown to man's estate, Ishmael takes first an Amalekite wife, but on her repudiation for a supposed insult to his father, and the expulsion of her tribe by an invading or migratory race from Yemen, he is united in marriage to a daughter of Modadh, the Jorhamite, chief of the strangers who occupy the country. Of this alliance twelve princes[3] are the issue, whose descendants and the tribes deriving their origin from them, are known by the name of "Mostaraba," *i.e.* naturalized or instititious Arabs, as

[1] "Call to mind when we gave the site of the house *of the Kaaba* for an abode unto Abraham, saying, Do not associate anything with me . . . and proclaim unto the people a solemn pilgrimage."—Koran, sura xxii. 27, 28.

[2] Black Stone at Mecca. This famous stone, which is a fragment of volcanic basalt, sprinkled with coloured crystals, is semicircular, and measures about six inches in height and eight inches in breadth. It is placed in the wall of the Kaaba, at the east outer corner, and about four feet from the ground. It has a border of silver round it. Its colour is reddish-black, and its surface is undulating and polished. Cf. Muir, ii. 35, and authorities quoted by Burckhardt, pp. 137, 138; Burton, vol. iii. 160-162, and 210; W. Irving, 16, 17.

[3] Genesis xvii. 20.

distinguished from the progeny of Kahtan, the same "with Joktan, the son of Eber, whom they name Al-Arab-al-Araba, genuine or pure Arabs."[1] Ishmael and the daughter of Modadh, the Jorhamite chief, are the reputed ancestors of Mahomet, the prophet of Mecca. "The ready pen of the traditionists has filled up the space of twenty-five centuries, between Ishmael and Mahomet, with a list of progenitors derived from Jewish sources; yet Mahomet himself never traced his pedigree higher than Adnân, and declared that all who went further back were guilty of fabrication and falsehood" (Muir, I. cxciii.).

Adnân was the father of Maadd, whose name was associated with the Maaddite tribes, the ancestors of the Coreish, who were in their different families descended from him. The year 130 B.C. is given as the date of Adnân's birth and from him, in the eighth generation, was descended Nadhr, born A.D. 134, the grandfather of Fehr Coreish, who was born A.D. 200.

Up to this time, under nine generations of kings of their race, the Jorhamites had enjoyed the supremacy in the Hejaz, and had *usurped* the privileges of the Kaaba, which, according to the language of the Moslems, belonged of right to the lineal descendants of Ishmael; when an immigrant tribe—the Azdites—from Yemen appeared, and, notwithstanding the opposition of the ruling race, were able successfully to establish themselves in Batn-Marr, a valley near Mecca. They did not, however, long remain there, but departed towards Syria, and left

[1] Sale, P. D., p. 8.

behind them a "remnant"—the Beni Khozaa, who settled in Mecca. These, with the Coreish, slaughtered or expelled from the country the Jorhamite families and their last king, Modadh. A struggle now commenced between the rival Maaddite houses for the administration of the Kaaba, and the supremacy at Mecca, but these were wrested from them by their former allies, the Beni Khozaa, and retained by them for upwards of two centuries; till after a variety of romantic adventures Cussai, the sixth in lineal descent from Fehr Coreish, after spending his youth in the highlands of Syria, returned to Mecca, married Hobba, the daughter of Holeil—the Khozaaite king—and was permitted to assume the immediate management of the Kaaba.

On the death of Holeil, Cussai set about, with the support of the other Coreish families, to assert and defend the *right* of his family to the guardianship of the Kaaba and the government of Mecca. Together with the guardianship of the temple, he possessed himself of the chief religious dignities connected with the sacerdotal office. From the Beni Sâfa he obtained the "Ijaza," or the right of dismissing the assembled Arab tribes from Minâ after the ceremonies of the Greater Pilgrimage; and, after much carnage, wrested from the Beni Khozaa the supremacy over the Hejaz. This took place about 440 A.D. Cussai gathered together, and settled at Mecca many scattered families of the Coreish, enlarged the town, built near the Kaaba the "Council House," where political questions were discussed and social ceremonies solemnized, and whence the yearly caravans set forth; and finally succeeded in establishing himself Sheikh of Mecca and Governor of the country.[1]

The dignities of which he possessed himself were five in number,—viz. (1) "The Hijaba," which gave him the keys and the control of the Kaaba; (2) "The Sicaya" and the "Rifada," or the prerogatives of providing drink and food for the pilgrims; (3) "The Kiyada," the command of the troops in war; (4) "The Liwa," the right of affixing the banner to the staff and presenting it to the standard-bearer; (5) "The Dar-ul-Nadwa," the presidency of the Hall of Council. The religious observances customary at the time of Cussai were those prevailing when Mahomet arose, and, the idols excepted, are there practised, with slight modifications, to this day. "The centre of veneration was the Kaaba, to visit which, to kiss the Black stone, and to make the seven circuits, was at all times regarded as a holy privilege" (Muir, i. ccv.).

Next was the Lesser Pilgrimage (Hajj al Asghar), which, in addition to the above, included the rite of running quickly to and fro seven times between the hills of Safa and Marwa close to

[1] Prideaux, "Life of Mahomet," p. 2, gives a different version of the method in which Cussai gained his position:—"Cosa was very famous among the Koreeshites for gaining to his family the keeping of the keys of the Caaba." "The government of Mecca and the presidency of the Caaba having fallen into the hands of Abu Gabshan, a weak and silly man, Cosa circumvented him while in a drunken humour, and bought of him the keys of the Temple, and with them, the presidency of it, for a bottle of wine."

the Kaaba.[1] This ceremony had especial merit in the holy month Rajab. Lastly, the Greater Pilgrimage (Hajj al Akbar) involving all the above and the additional rite of pilgrimage to Arafat—an eminence of granite rocks, ten or twelve miles east of Mecca. This can be performed only in the holy month "Dzul Hijja." On the 8th the pilgrims start from Mecca, spend the 9th at Arafat, and on the same evening hurry back to a spot called Mosdalifa. Two or three succeeding days are spent at Minâ, and the pilgrimage is concluded with the sacrifice of a victim.[2]

The country round Mecca to a distance of several miles was called sacred (Haram), and during four months of the year, by general consent, wars and hostilities were laid aside, so that the pilgrims could travel unmolested from distant parts, and, assuming the sacred garb (Ihram), perform the accustomed rites in peace and security.

It will be gathered from the above how strangely the idolatrous practices at the Kaaba were mixed up with the biblical story of Abraham, Hagar, and Ishmael, to whom the traditions current among the Arabs long before the era of Mahomet attributed the first founding of the temple and its rites. Doubtless this legend may be dismissed into the realms of fancy,

[1] This act was supposed to be in memory of the distressed mother Hagar, anxiously running in search of water for her son before the waters of Zem Zem were miraculously brought to light in answer to her cry.

[2] Muir, I. ccvi. *Vide* Life of Burckhardt, "Chambers's Miscellany," vol. x. No. 4, where an interesting account of the ceremonies of the yearly pilgrimage is given.—Burton, M. and M., vol. iii.

as devoid of consistency; but the question arises how the worship at Mecca came to be what it was at the time of Mahomet's birth. The worship was made up of two totally different elements; viz. pure idolatry and, in addition, rites and observances which, by tradition, were associated with the story of living characters of the Old Testament, and the reality of that association riveted and certified by the names of spots in the neighbourhood which could be seen and visited, and which were intimately connected with the ceremonies which were performed.

The following is probably the way in which the above came about. It may be assumed that the purely idolatrous practices, the reverence for the well Zem Zem and the Black stone and the circuits of the Kaaba, &c. were of indigenous growth, or were imported by the tribes and peoples of Yemen who settled at Mecca. This place owed its importance as a large commercial centre to its position on the western caravan route, midway between Yemen and Petra, and to its plentiful supply of water.[1] Here, it is pointed out, a change of carriage eventually took place, the merchandise for the north and south dividing at this point, and occasioning thus a per manent intercourse between it and Syria, Egypt, and the ports of South Arabia. It is easy to imagine that merchants of various nationalities, and from distant parts, would from time to time visit the great entrepot at Mecca, and that the Bedouins of Central

[1] The well Zem Zem is about seven feet eight inches in diameter and fifty-six feet deep to the surface of the water. The water is said to be very abundant and wholesome, though its taste is brackish.

Arabia, attracted to the spot, would give to the shrine, its well, and its worship, a kind of national or metropolitan character; and that the superstitious reverence for the place prevalent throughout the peninsula would continue long after its commercial pre-eminence had, with the failure of the caravan trade, ceased. The traditional belief in the Abrahamic origin of the Kaaba which is asserted in the Koran (sura ii. 118, *et seq.*) is probably to be accounted for by the early and extensive commingling of the Abrahamic stocks with the other Semitic tribes chiefly settled in Yemen. Branches of the descendants of Ishmael settled, as has been shown, about and to the north of Mecca; and these, with the Nabatheans, a great commercial nation who had been attracted by its good business position, brought with them to their new settlement the Abrahamic legends, which the Jews who traded there, and who were settled in considerable force in the country, tended to revive and perpetuate. Thus in time the Abrahamic story and the Jewish legends were grafted on to the indigenous idol-worship and became incorporated with it. Hence it was that the well Zem Zem became the scene of Hagar's relief; hence the sacrifice in the valley of Mina to typify the vicarious sacrifice offered by Abraham in place of his son *Ishmael;* hence Abraham and Ishmael were made the founders of their temple, which, under the sanction of the name of the Father of the Faithful and the Friend of God, was, in the belief of the followers of Islam, to be established as a house of prayer for all nations.[1]

Cussai having thus concentrated in his own

[1] The above account of the origin of the worship of the Kaaba and its ceremonies is adopted from Sir W. Muir, i. cap. iii. sec. iv.

person the chief temporal and spiritual dignities at Mecca, died, leaving three sons, viz. Abd-al-Dâr, Abd-Menâf, and Abd-al-Ozza.[1] To his eldest son he left all the offices which he held; but Abd-al-Dâr, less energetic than Abd-Menâf, allowed the latter to usurp the real management of public affairs. On the death of Abd-al-Dâr, his rights passed to his sons and grandsons; but the latter were too young to sustain successfully their legal prerogatives against their more powerful rivals, Al-Muttalib, Hashim, Abd-Shams, and Naufal, the sons of Abd-Menâf. Two hostile factions thus arose in Mecca, and bloodshed was avoided only by a compromise, which, securing the other offices to the elder branch of the family, gave the privilege of providing food and water to Hashim, and the leadership in war to his younger brother, Abd-Shams.

The noble and generous character of Hashim and his riches prompted and enabled him munificently to perform the duties of the sacred offices he had thus obtained. Reservoirs of water were by his care provided for the pilgrims, and food liberally supplied them. He is said to have fed the people of Mecca during a famine. Commercial treaties were concluded by him or his brothers with the neighbouring powers—with the Roman emperor, the ruler of Abyssinia, the king of Persia, and the princes of Himyar, in Yemen. By Salm, a widow of Medina, of the tribe of Khazraj, he had a son born in his old age (A.D. 497), who was soon after left an orphan

[1] His two sons, Menaf and Ozza, were called after his gods. From the latter was descended Khadija, daughter of Khuweilid, and wife of Mahomet.

by the death of his father at Gaza. The dignified offices which he held were bequeathed to his elder brother, Al Muttalib, who, with loyal affection, succeeded before his death, notwithstanding the efforts and opposition of the rival race of Abd Shams, in reinstating the orphan boy in his paternal estate, which had been appropriated by his uncle Naufal; and under the name of Abd-al-Muttalib, the son of Hashim became the head of the Coreish in Mecca.

Succeeding thus to the dignified office of providing food and drink to the pilgrims, Abd-al-Muttalib had to contend against the continual rivalry and opposition of the richer, and probably more powerful, family of Omeya, the son of Abd Shams, who, as we have seen, held the important office of the Leadership in war. But his fortunate rediscovery of the ancient well Zem Zem, which for some centuries had been lost or choked up, in restoring to Mecca its abundant supply of water, strengthened his influence, which was further increased by the possession of a large and powerful family of ten sons and six daughters, so that he continued to his death the virtual chief of Mecca.

Of his sons, the most important in the subsequent history of their race were Al-Harith, his first-born, Al-Zobier, Abu-Talib, Abu-Lahab, and the youngest, Abdallah, who was born in the year A.D. 545.[1] It was during his tenure of office as chief of the Kaaba (A.D. 570) that Abraha, the viceroy of Yemen, sought, in the interest of the Christian temple at Sanā, to de-

[1] At a later period two other sons were born to him, viz., Abbas and Hamza, both of whom play a conspicuous part in the subsequent history of the establishment of Islam. Hamza was in all probability born about the same time as Mahomet.

stroy its formidable rival at Mecca. The failure of this expedition, and the dignified conduct of Abd-al-Muttalib, contributed much to the confirmation of his power.

But a few months before the invasion of Abraha, "the year of the Elephant" (A.D. 570), Abd-al-Muttalib had betrothed his son Abdallah to a maiden of the house of Coreish, Amina, the daughter of Wahb, the son of Abd-Menaf, the son of Zohra, a brother of that famous Cussai who, more than a hundred years before, had consolidated the fortunes of their house. Abdallah was the best-beloved son of his father, a child of benediction, who being once in fulfilment of a vow devoted to death, like his storied ancestor Ishmael, on the heights of Arafat, had, at the eleventh hour, been saved from the sacrificial fire and given again to life. For Abd-al-Muttalib had promised, if the Almighty would give him ten sons, that one of them should be devoted; and it was only after the divining arrows[1] had ten times been cast that the slaughter of one hundred camels before the idol god was permitted to redeem the victim and absolve the parent from his rash vow.[2]

[1] Conf. Koran, sura v. 4; and Sale's P. D., sec. v.

[2] Thus Mahometans report their prophet to have said that he was the *son of two sacrifices*, meaning (1) his father Abdallah, and (2) as being descended from Ishmael, which son, and not Isaac, they believe Abraham to have offered.—Conf. Sale's Koran, cap. xxxvii. p. 369; Muir, i. cap. 4.

CHAPTER III.

BIRTH OF MAHOMET, AND LIFE TO HIS FORTIETH YEAR.—[A.D. 570–610.]

BRIEF was the wedded life of Abdallah and Amina. Shortly after the marriage her husband set out with the yearly caravan for Gaza, in South Syria, leaving pregnant the young wife who was destined to see him no more. It was their first and last parting, for on the return journey Abdallah sickened, and being left with his grand maternal relatives at Medina, died and was buried there. For the support of his widow he left behind him no richer legacy than four camels, a flock of goats, and a slave girl named Baraka. Wonderful stories are told of the marvels which accompanied the gestation and birth of his infant child. The very powers of the air were shaken to herald his advent. All oracles were dumb, the sacred fire of Zoroaster, guarded for centuries by the Magi, was extinguished before the greater light which had dawned. The evil spirits which dwell in malignant stars were abashed, and fled shrieking, and Eblis himself was hurled into the depths of the sea! Many legendary tales, which resemble those told of our Blessed Saviour in the apocryphal Gospels, are related about, and associated with, the infant son of Amina, whose birth, with the nearest approach to accuracy, is fixed for the autumn of the year A.D. 570.[1]

Under the rocks of the Abu-Cobeis, which rise eastward of Mecca over the narrow valley, stood the house of Amina, the birthplace of her only son. At the time of the infant's birth, the aged Abd-al-Muttalib was worshipping in the Kaaba; and, taking the child to the sacred shrine, like Simeon of old, he lifted him up in his arms, and blessed God and gave thanks, saying, that he was to be called "Mohammad," a name in not unfamiliar use before and at the time.[2] But Amina had not long the comfort of her son's presence. It was then customary for the infants of her house to be nurtured among the outlying Bedouin tribes. Moreover, grief is said to have dried up the fountain of her breast, and she was thus, for a double reason, constrained to part with her son, who, amidst the valleys and hills which range southward of Tayif, with his nurse Halima, breathed the pure air of the desert. Here, too, he learned the purer speech of Arabia among the Beni-Saâd, to which tribe his foster-mother belonged, and for which he afterwards entertained the greatest affection and gratitude.

Strange stories, as usual, are made to surround the infant child in his mountain home. The house of Halima is blessed for his sake; her flocks and herds are, beyond hope, prolific amid the green pastures where they lie down, and where the still waters never fail. The child, too, grows and increases in favour with all; and, more than this, the heavenly

[1] Conf. W. Irving, pp. 12, 13; Muir, ii. p. 12.

[2] Muir, ii. p. 16, and note.

messengers are sent, and, at God's command, wring from his heart the single black drop of original sin, and, so purified and gifted with the prophetic light, he is thus early selected by the Almighty to be the future channel to man of the last and best revelation of His will.[1]

At the end of two years the infant was weaned and sent to visit his mother, but the latter, whilst charmed at his healthy looks, and dreading the unwholesome air of Mecca, sent him back to his mountain home with his nurse, who had so faithfully watched over him. When approaching his fifth year, he appears to have become subject to certain epileptic fits, which alarmed his foster-parents, as such attacks were attributed to the influence of evil spirits, and made them resolve to rid themselves of their charge. So he was again taken to his mother, and the reason of the visit explained to her; and though persuaded to continue their guardianship for some time longer, they finally restored him to Amina when he had reached his fifth year.

[1] It would be manifestly unfair to make Mahomet or *his* doctrine answerable for all the miraculous incidents which have clustered round nearly every event of his life. To the Koran alone can we look for the only correct exposition of his views. Some of the stories which occur in the events of his life are so beautiful, that it is certainly a matter of regret to be obliged to pronounce them devoid of historical value. The passage (sura xciv. 1), "Have we not opened thy breast and eased thee of thy burden?" is thought by some to allude to the above story; but it is more probable that the text itself gave rise to the subsequently-framed interpretation. Conf. Koran (sura xlvii. 21), where Mahomet is directed to ask pardon for his sins, thus acknowledging himself to be a sinner. (*Vide* Sale's note *ad loc.*)

In his sixth year (A.D. 575) he paid a visit to Yathrib, better known by its later name of Medina. There he saw the tomb of his father, and found youthful relatives of a companionable age. At Abwâ, a spot halfway from Medina to his native place, he had the misfortune to lose his sole remaining parent. Though the sorrows and griefs of childhood are happily brief and evanescent, time appears never to have obliterated the memory of his mother, nor the feeling of desolation which her loss occasioned him. Years subsequently, after his prophetic mission had been preached and accepted, he visited her tomb, and there lifted up his voice and wept, and especially did he mourn that the Almighty would not permit him to pray for the parent he so tenderly loved, inasmuch as she had died in unbelief, and ignorant of that saving faith which her son was sent to proclaim.

The faithful slave Baraka escorted him back to Mecca, and there, in the house of his grandfather, the little orphan found for two years a happy home; and when Abd-al-Muttalib died (A.D. 578) he consigned to his son Abu-Talib the charge of the boy. In the family of his uncle he was treated as a son, and faithfully, as we shall see, did the generous Abu-Talib, in adversity, and through evil and good report, fulfil the sacred trust imposed upon him.

Living thus in the house of his grandfather and uncle from his sixth year, the youthful mind of Mahomet cannot but have imbibed lasting and important impressions, from the domestic and social circumstances by which, at his susceptible age, he was surrounded. Abd-al-Muttalib was the Chief of

Mecca, and fulfilled, as his father had before him, the most important of the sacerdotal offices connected with the national worship. To him for food and help resorted the devout pilgrim from his distant home, and in his hands was the custody of the sacred well Zem Zem. We read, too, that with the other chiefs of his family in Mecca he was wont daily to spend some time beneath the shadow of the Kaaba, and that the youthful Mahomet was there his constant companion. The grave and dignified manners and words of the old patriarch, daily association with the ceremonies of the holy house, the superstitious awe which surrounded the place, the prostrations, the prayers, and the pious offerings of the faithful, his own near relationship to the priestly families, the order and decorum of the house of his guardians, where the sacred rites were rigidly observed, all these together doubtless strongly and lastingly influenced him, and gave that tendency to his thoughts which manifested itself in the prophetic character he afterwards assumed.[1]

To the sacred offices held by Abd-al-Muttalib, Zobier, his second son, succeeded (for the eldest, Al-Harith, was dead), and from him they descended to Abu Talib; but he was poor and unable to meet

[1] Note, "Among the religious observances of the Arabs in their 'days of ignorance'—that is to say, before the promulgation of the Moslem doctrines—fasting and prayer had a foremost place. They had three principal fasts within the year: one of seven, one of nine, and one of thirty days. They prayed three times a day: about sunrise, at noon, and about sunset; turning their faces in the direction of the Kaaba, which was their Kebla, or point of adoration."—W. Irving, "Life of Mahomet," p. 17.

the demands which the performance of the hospitable duties involved, and so the privilege of supplying water was made over to Abbas, a younger and richer brother; whilst the right of giving food to the pilgrims was made over to the descendants of Naufal, a brother of the munificent Hashim. Still, from the nobility of his character, and the gentleness yet firmness of his disposition, Abu Talib occupied a commanding position among the richer chiefs of Mecca as one of the guardians of the Kaaba, though his positive power was less than that of the richer descendants of Abd-Shams. The latter was the father of Omeya, from whom the royal race of the Omeyades took their name. Omeya was the father of Harb, and Harb of Abu Sofian, afterwards the obstinate opponent and bitter enemy of Mahomet.

It was unfortunate for the preservation of the rights of private property, and the orderly execution of the law, that the powers of the government had thus become divided among the hostile, or, at any rate, rival branches of the house of Coreish; for the consequence was that there remained no single chief in Mecca strong enough to restrain tyranny and oppression, and to protect the helpless. The inconvenience of this state of things, which threatened seriously to interfere with the commercial prosperity of the city, led in time to the formation of a league among the heads of the chief families, called the "Hilf-al-Fadhul," the object of which was to secure the due and impartial execution of justice. [1]

The arrival of the early caravan on its way

[1] Muir, ii. 10.

from the south to Syria, with the influx of the pilgrims to the Kaaba, was probably the most interesting event of the year, and was looked forward to with ardent curiosity by the youth of Mecca. The multitude of camels bearing spices, the merchants of Aden and Hadhramaut with their precious freights—the choice products of Yemen and of India—the bustle and tumult of the crowded streets, would excite the imagination with visions of those distant regions whence all the riches came, and arouse a desire to visit them. From this influence the youthful Mahomet did not escape. At his earnest entreaty his guardian, Abu Talib (who, like most of the chiefs of his house, engaged in mercantile adventure), permitted the youth, then in his twelfth year, to accompany him on the northward journey. On this, and on subsequent trading expeditions, indelible impressions must have been made upon his youthful mind. With the exception of one visit to Medina when six years of age, and his infant days spent in his desert home in the hills of Tayif, he had never been absent from the narrow valley of Mecca. Now the daily march, the nightly halt, new scenes, the camp fires, around which wild tales and legends of spectral beings haunting each hill and vale, and of ancient races swept away in ages past, [1] would naturally imprint themselves deeply on the imagination of the melancholy child. On the way he had to journey between the mountains and the sea, and would pass, not without mournful regret, the tomb of his mother at Abwâ; and then on to Akaba,

[1] Conf. Koran, sura lxxxix. 6; sura xci. 11; sura vii. 63-73; sura liv. 18-31; and Sale's P. D., p. 67.

where, in the dim distance of the western sky, there would arise to his view the sacred heights of Horeb and of Sinai, once the scene of God's message to man through that mighty Prophet, to whom in after-years he ventured to deem himself more than equal. He would visit the rocks of Petra, the glories of which had passed away; and so to the halting-place at Bostra, beyond the accursed valley, where the waters of the Dead Sea were said to hide for ever the devoted cities of the plain.

During these journeys Mahomet must without doubt have come in contact with numerous Christians, who, as we have before stated, were scattered over the regions he visited; and it is not improbable that he may frequently have witnessed the ceremonies of their worship. The Christian Church in the East had been for a long time convulsed by theological controversies. Bitter disputes for centuries over the great mysteries of the faith had ended in the production of a number of sects. There were the Arians, who denied the essential equality of the three Persons of the Godhead; the Sabellians, who reduced these Persons to three relations; and the Eutychians, who believed in the fusion of the Godhead and the manhood of Christ into one nature. There were the Jacobites, adherents of the Monophysite heresy, the Nazaræans, and the Ebionites, numerous in Arabia, the Marianites, who made the Virgin Mother the third person in the Trinity; the Collyridians, who made Mary their God, and worshipped her as such;[1]

[1] Koran, sura v. 115: "And when God shall say unto Jesus at the last day, O Jesus, Son of Mary, hast thou said unto

and "other sects there were, of many denominations, within the borders of Arabia, which took refuge there from the proscription of the imperial edicts" (Sale, p. 35). We learn, too, that the worship of saints and images had there arrived at a very high pitch, and that many other superstitions largely prevailed (Sale, P.D., p. 33).

In Syria, Mahomet would see the Christian religion the ruling national faith, in full vigour, with its scenic ritual, its crosses, pictures, vestments, processions, and regularly-recurring services; and these observances he would, doubtless, compare with that gross idolatry, in the practice of which he had grown up to years of manhood. Still, though those who called themselves by the name of the Saviour were numerous in Arabia, in Syria, at Bostra, and at Hira, and though he must have had full and ample opportunity of learning the truth of the things which they believed, "nothing is more remarkable than the gross ignorance of some of the leading features of Christianity, which, notwithstanding all the means of information which, at any rate during his residence at Medina, he possessed, is displayed by Mahomet" (Muir, I. cxci. note).

In the account of his first journey, in his twelfth year, miraculous signs crowd upon us, and the visible protection of Heaven accompanies the youthful prophet. At one time the wings of his guardian angel shield him from the noonday heat; at another, the

men, take me and my mother for two gods, beside God?" From this passage it is evident that this early worship of Mary was known to Mahomet.

withered trees of the desert are clothed in living green, to afford shelter to the chosen of Heaven (W. Irving, p. 20). At Bostra, a city lying eastward of the Jordan, and chiefly inhabited by Nestorian Christians, where the caravan halted, the prophetic light which shone in his face, and the seal of prophecy between his shoulders, are seen and recognized by a monk of a neighbouring convent. By him the youth is hospitably entertained and instructed in the true faith of the living God; but especially, and thus early, is there sown in his heart a deep-rooted abhorrence of that idolatry in which he had hitherto been educated.[2]

This Nestorian monk is variously called Bahîra, Sergius or Jergîs, Felix and Said, and the whole story is so mixed up with fable as to make it, as it stands, quite unworthy of belief. It is quite possible that Mahomet may have imbibed impressions, or received instruction similar to that noted in the text, during one of his commercial visits to the Syrian towns; and we are further assured that he was on intimate and familiar terms with several persons of the Christian and Jewish faith. It appears a vain and unprofitable task to inquire at what particular time he adopted his iconoclastic views, and was led to assert his especial dogma of the unity of the Godhead. The most superficial acquaintance with the books of the

[1] This is an old myth, and occurs in the story of the lambent flame which played in the hair of Ascanius, and that settled on the cradle of Servius Tullius (Livy, i. 35).

[2] Prideaux, "Life of Mahomet," p. 7; Muir, i. 36, note; Lamartine, i. p. 91; Dr. Sprenger, "Life of Mahomet," p. 79; W. Irving, p. 21. Conf. also Sale, Koran, sura xvi. p. 223, where the question is discussed.

Old Testament—such knowledge as he had full and ample opportunity of gaining, would impress on his mind the great salient fact that idolatry and the worship of strange gods was the one especial sin which uniformly provoked the wrath of Heaven, and called down temporal punishment upon that chosen nation, whose especial mission it was to keep alive in the earth the knowledge of Him in whose worship no graven image was to take part. If we can assume his acquaintance with the first two Mosaic commandments, or if he had learnt the "Shema" (Deut. vi. 4) usually taught to Jewish children, even of the humble classes,[1] we have sufficient data to account for the two special doctrines which he sought afterwards to enforce.[2]

At the annual fair at Ocatz, which he attended, there is reason to believe that he listened to the fervid eloquence and pure doctrine preached by Coss, the Christian bishop of Najran, and there he may have

[1] Farrar, "Life of Christ," i. 89, note.

[2] On this head Dr. Adler, Chief Rabbi, has kindly favoured me with the following remarks, in answer to an inquiry whether the Decalogue formed part of the daily services of the Jews at that time. He says: "At the time when he (Mahomet) lived, it is probable that the recitation of the Decalogue did not form an integral portion of the daily public service; for we are told that the priests recited it at the Temple service, but that laymen were not to include it in their daily devotions, lest they should imagine that these were the only precepts given in the law. (Talmud Berachoth.) Still the Decalogue is included in every prayer-book, and was read as the lesson of the day on the Feast of Pentecost, and on two Sabbaths of the year. Mahomet would have become acquainted with the prohibitions of images from his intercourse with Jews."

imbibed the germs of that faith round which the tribes of Arabia were one day to rally. The mutual animosity of Jew towards Christian, though both professed to worship the true God, though both appealed to the Old Testament, and both equally revered the name of Abraham and professed to abhor that idolatry in which he had been bred, may have led him to think that possibly some divine truth lay hid in both these systems of belief, though covered and concealed by human inventions, and may have suggested to him the possibility of forming out of these conflicting elements one single simple catholic creed, and of thus uniting mankind in the worship and love of the Great Father of all.

And so the life of Mahomet ran on. At the age of twenty (A.D. 590) he is found engaged in what is called "Fijar," or "the Sacrilegious War," in which "he was present with his uncles and discharged arrows at the enemy."[1] This arose from a feud between the Coreish and the Beni Hawazin, a tribe of kindred origin, and gained its name from having been fought within the sacred territory and during one of the sacred months. At this time, too, he was employed, like Moses and David of old, in tending sheep, and in following the ewes great with young, in the valley beneath the slopes of the Jebel Jyad, south of Mecca. Such an occupation was suited to the contemplative and thoughtful mind of the youth, whose pure manners and unobtrusive demeanour gained him the title of "Al-Amin," or "the Faithful."

When he had reached his twenty-fifth year, on

[1] Muir, ii. 6.

the recommendation of Abu Talib, he entered the service of Khadija, a rich widow of Mecca. She was of the house of Coreish, the daughter of Khuweilid, who was the son of Asad, the son of Abd-al-Ozza, the son of Cussai. With Meisara, her servant, he was placed in charge of the widows' merchandise; and accompanying the yearly caravan to the north, by judicious barter with the Syrian merchants of Bostra, Aleppo, and Damascus, succeeded in doubling Khadija's venture. From Marr-al-Tzahran, the last halting-place on the return journey before Mecca, he was sent forward to announce to his thrifty and expectant mistress the success of their journey. The widow was charmed with the noble features of the ingenuous youth, and her heart was touched with a soft and irresistible feeling. The negotiations and advances which her love and modesty set on foot soon brought about the union she desired. The home of Mahomet and Khadija was a bright and happy one, and their marriage fortunate and fruitful. Two sons and four daughters were its issue. Their eldest son was Casim, who died at the age of two years; then followed (in what precise order is unknown) four daughters,—Zeinab, Rockeya, Om-Kolthum, and Fatima; and lastly a son, generally known by the name of Abdallah, who died in infancy.

The wealth of Khadija raised Mahomet to a level with the other chiefs of his house, and relieved him from the shepherd's crook and from his duties among the camel-drivers of Mecca. The love of Khadija, who had at first been attracted by his noble and pleasing exterior, increased daily at the recognition of the sterling qualities which her partial heart was ready to discover in the husband of her choice. Though usually reserved and thoughtful, he was known at times to unbend, and to yield to a vein of humour, which occasionally tinged his graver words. He was able to keep his passions under the strongest control, and in his general intercourse amongst his friends, the affectionate though often hidden impulses of his heart knew how to "grapple with hooks of steel" those whom his commanding aspect at first had awed and attracted. But the chief idiosyncrasy of his character was a quiet patient determination of will and fixedness of purpose, which neither years of opposition nor personal danger nor exile could subdue, and which "was destined to achieve the marvellous work of bowing towards him the hearts of all Arabia as the heart of one man" (Muir, ii. 31).

In all his troubles, and amid all his mental doubts and conflicts, he had one tender and affectionate bosom into which he could pour his griefs, and to which he could, in later years, confide the story of the ecstatic visions which, in the solitary cave or on the arid uplands, haunted his day dreams and his nightly vigils. For the heart of Mahomet did safely trust her, and Khadija yielded to him her faith; and when the world called him impostor and cheat, she was the first to acknowledge him to be indeed the apostle of God.

In his thirty-fifth year, the Kaaba having been seriously injured by the action of one of those periodic deluges to which the valley of Mecca is to the present day liable, the chiefs of the Coreish set about the task of executing the necessary repairs, for which the timbers of a ship stranded on the coast near Jedda furnished them a welcome though unexpected supply of material. The rivalry and jealousy of the various "heads of houses" in Mecca who exercised any of the sacerdotal offices was so great that an elaborate previous distribution of the work was necessary before the repairs were allowed to be undertaken. At length the four sides of the shrine were divided among four sets of the families interested, and then they began their task. The fiery Walid [1] was the first to commence the work, but as it proceeded, and the walls rose, the question presented itself who was to move to its place the sacred Black Stone. The dispute grew hot, swords were drawn, and bloodshed was imminent, when it was settled to refer the solution of the dispute to him who first entered the sacred inclosure by the gate of the Beni-Sheyba; when lo! Mahomet was seen approaching, and was the first to reach the appointed spot. The story goes on to tell how he spread his mantle on the ground, placed the stone thereon, and gave to the chief of each party a corner, so that each might equally assist in raising it, but that he himself guided and fixed it in its final resting-place.

We cannot but suppose that this incident, accompanied by the circumstances which assigned to him the most honourable task in the rehabilitation of the national shrine, was deeply impressed on his memory; and that it afterwards served to confirm his own

[1] Walid-Ibn-al-Mughira was descended from Makhzum, a son of Yokdah, uncle of Cussai.

belief in the divineness of his mission, and strengthened his claim on the faith of his adherents.

Though after his marriage with Khadija he still continued his commercial pursuits, and at times accompanied the yearly caravans north and south, and visited the fairs of Arabia, he yet had ample leisure for that religious meditation to which he was naturally inclined. The general bias of his mind in this direction, fostered by his early training and associations in the house of Abd-al-Muttalib and of Abu Talib, inclined him to speculation in matters of faith; and this was further stimulated by the view of the gross idolatry which he saw practised at the Kaaba, as contrasted with the more spiritual worship of the Christian and Jew, of which he had been witness on his visits to Syria. With the real doctrines and true teaching of neither of these religions had he made himself acquainted. He knew not how in the eternal purpose of God the ritual of the Mosaic dispensation, its hallowed priesthood, its bleeding sacrifices, its lamb without spot or blemish, the blood sprinkled on the mercy-seat, were types and shadows of Him who was to come. Of the need of a *Redeemer*, and of the finished *Atonement*, he knew nothing; and he doubtless formed his opinion of the Christian religion and of the Jewish Church chiefly from corrupt Christian sects who paid adoration to the Virgin Mary and to saints and images, and from the Jewish communities he met on his journeys, and whom he considered no less idolatrous. With such erroneous notions, and the sight of the mutual hatred, the divergent worship and recriminations alike of Jew and Gentile, it is scarcely to be marvelled at that the necessity for some reformation occurred to him; and that his solitary musings aided him in fixing his mind on the task which he set before himself of freeing the observances of religion from all visible objects of idolatrous adoration, and of reducing the faith of the creature to its original purity, the sum and substance of which was to be the worship of the one only God.

Such were probably some of the thoughts which occupied him; but other influences there were at work which further directed his mind in this field of speculation. In the house of Khadija, Waraca, her cousin, was a frequent and a welcome visitor. He is said to have been a convert to Christianity, and to have had some knowledge of the Scriptures of both Christian and Jew. From him Mahomet is "thought to have derived much of his information regarding these writings, and many of the traditions of the Mishna and Talmud, on which he draws so copiously in the Koran."[1] From Zeid also,[2] his adopted son, sprung from Arab tribes in which Christianity had made considerable progress, he would gather some dim impressions of the teachings of the Christian faith; and Othman,[3] too, another cousin of Khadija, who had embraced Christianity at Constantinople,

[1] W. Irving, "Life of Mahomet," p. 29.

[2] For his previous history, see Muir, ii. 47.

[3] Othman Ibn-Huweirith, cousin of Khadija. He was put to death at Constantinople. He is not to be confounded with Othman-Ibn-Affan, afterwards Caliph.

would further instruct him in the chief tenets which he held.

From the knowledge thus gained by actual intercourse with those who had been instructed, however imperfectly, in a better faith: from the general spirit of inquiry which is said to have prevailed at the time; from what he himself had seen and learnt of the nature of Christian and Jewish worship, and from dim traditions of the purer faith of their ancestor Abraham, he gradually became sensible how much such pure adoration was at variance with the gross and degrading idolatry which prevailed in Arabia. With a brooding anxiety for something that would answer the secret longings of his soul, he began to withdraw himself from the busy scenes of the city to the barren hills, whose desolate solitudes were congenial to his meditative and melancholy nature.

We read that often with his faithful wife he repaired to the cave of Hirâ[1] for meditation and prayer, and that his long and anxious vigils and nightly wanderings were followed by ecstasies, and trances, and convulsive fits long continued, which alarmed his wife, but in which "the faithful" see the beginning of the working of the Spirit of God, and the throes of a mind burdened with a revelation more than human. His tendency to epileptic attacks, and his long vigils, sufficiently account for these pheno-

[1] Mount Hirâ lies about three miles north of Mecca, and is about a quarter of a league to the left of the road to Arafat, and beyond the Sherifs' summer-house. The cave is about four yards long, and varies in breadth from one to three yards (*vide* Muir, ii. 55, notes).

mena. To the faithful, however, they constituted the ordeal through which he had to pass before he could be made the means of revealing the message of Heaven.

It is not easy for an adherent of any other religion to form an impartial opinion upon the part played by the founder of Islam. Of those who deny the truth of the claims which Mahomet sets forth, the judgments have been, and probably will continue to be, very divergent. Luther looked upon him as "a devil and the firstborn child of Satan." The gentle Melanchthon considered "that Mahomet was inspired by Satan, because he does not explain what sin is, and showeth not the reason of human misery." Maracci, on the Papal side, was of opinion that Mahometanism and Lutheranism were not very dissimilar,—"witness the iconoclastic tendencies of both." Spanheim and D'Herbelot were liberal in their epithets of "wicked impostor," "dastardly liar," &c., with reference to him.[1] By one earnest and learned writer [2] he is pronounced a wilful and intentional deceiver from first to last, who, for the purpose of raising himself to supreme power, invented the wicked imposture which he palmed with so much success on the world. He is accused, in prosecution of his design, of having abandoned a licentious course of life, and of having affected that of an Eremite, in order to gain "a reputation for sanctity before he set up for prophet"; and with his accomplices in the cave, of having "made his Al-Koran" whilst pretending that his visits there were for fasting

[1] Quarterly Review, October, 1869.

[2] Prideaux, "Life of Mahomet," pp. 11, 110.

and prayer; and generally that hypocrisy, the lust of power, and lechery were the sole and leading principles of his conduct. Such indiscriminate abuse is unsupported by facts, and cannot be justified by a reference to what is known of his early conduct. His life up to the time of his assumption of the prophetic character is eminently decorous, for "all authorities agree in ascribing to the youth of Mahomet a correctness of deportment and a purity of manners rare among the people of Mecca." [1]

Happily the time has come when the use of bitter epithets, and the sweeping condemnation of those who agree not with us, are no longer demanded in religious controversies. Critics of the present age are men of greater enlightenment, of truer education, and of a charity that weighs in a juster balance the motive and deeds of those mighty men who for good or for evil have graven their names on the page of history. A recent writer [2] rejoices that justice can now be dealt to Mahomet without fear of misconception or misrepresentation. "It is no longer thought," he says, "any part of the duty of a Christian writer to see nothing but wickedness and imposture in the author of the great antagonistic creed."

His domestic conduct was that of a faithful and affectionate husband, whilst his reserved, meditative, and sober manners in public secured him the love and praise of his fellow-townsmen. It is impossible to suppose, if his conduct and character

[1] Muir, ii. 14.

[2] Freeman, "History of the Saracens," p. 38.

had been licentious and hypocritical, that the reputation which he established and maintained would have been as high and faultless as it was. Judging his motives by his acts, and by those parts of the Koran which he first promulgated, our view of Mahomet will at once differ from those who admit his loftiest claims, and from those who denounce him as the worst and most successful impostor the world has seen. We shall see in him the picture of a soul at first honestly searching for the light amid ecstatic visions of heaven and hell, under conviction of the unity of God, and of His beneficent kindness, and persuaded that the raging fire and the pit were for those whose balances were not heavy with good deeds;[1] of one believing in the future judgment of the righteous God;[2] and in the fate of those nations, the children of Ad and the Thamudites, who multiplied corruptions on the earth, and were swept away for their rejection of the Lord and His apostles.[3] Amid such visions and fancies, groping his way to a purer faith, he at length came to believe that the trances and mental paroxysms, which drove him to meditate suicide,[4] were the true working of the same God who in ages past had inspired other messengers, and now had selected him for the same high office.

[1] Koran, sura ci. 1–8.

[2] Sura xcv.

[3] Sura lxxxiv. 1–8. Muir thinks that at this period his speculations unburdened themselves in wild and impassioned verses, and that these were afterwards embodied and preserved in the Koran.

[4] He was about to throw himself from Mount Thubeir, but was arrested by a voice from heaven (Muir, ii. 84).

Such a thought once harboured in his soul, the idea of a "Divine commission" would soon be fully formed, grow strong, and be identified with his desire to give to his native land a purer faith; and then, almost unconsciously, the demon of spiritual pride and ambition would begin its subtle work, and thus "at this crisis the fate of Mahomet and of Islam trembled in the balance. It was his hour of trial, and he fell" (Muir, ii. 93).

Assuming that his early longings after a more spiritual faith, and his searchings after God were earnest and real, the Christian scholar who contemplates him at this, the turning point of his career, will view with regret the melancholy result of his aspirations. For it is hard to believe that the Spirit of Truth leaves in darkness and error the honest heart which looks to Him for light. If Mahomet's sole purpose had been the search after truth, if his eye had been single, the still small voice would have doubtless suggested the way; some Philip, in his desert Gaza, would have pointed him to the true Light; the teaching, which the great Apostle of the Gentiles found in that land of Arabia, would have been his also, and Mahomet might have become a bright herald of the cross to its idolatrous tribes. But the stealthy advances of a worldly ambition blinded his mental vision, blunted his dependence on a higher Power, and by the suggestions of the Evil One took captive his soul, and chained it in that delusive, yet strong and unwavering belief, which swayed his future career, and retained a paramount influence over him to the hour of his death,—that he was the ordained of Heaven, the messenger of God. "Thus was Mahomet, by whatever deceptive process led to the high blasphemy of forging the name of God, a crime repeatedly stigmatized in the Coran itself as the greatest that mankind can commit" (Muir, ii. 75).

That his own belief in his Divine mission was a real, and apparently (however much he was deceived) an honest one, and yet that spiritual pride and ambition was the rock upon which he split, will abundantly appear from a careful consideration of those motives which usually influence men in the prosecution of any great object in life. Riches he sought not, for his marriage had placed him on a level with the wealthy chiefs of Mecca, and gave him more than sufficient to supply his moderate wants. We shall find afterwards, when riches untold might have been his, that he maintained the same simplicity of manners which had ever distinguished him. Regal state he coveted not; for when his name was exalted above the name of all creatures, borne on the prayers of the faithful, and made second only to Allah himself, he still occupied the same humble house, at times performed even the menial duties of his household, still exercised himself in acts of humility, and still expressed himself as much as ever in need of the mercy of the All-Compassionate for his entrance into Paradise.[1] And, finally, ambition could hardly have been altogether his prevailing motive, for he made no provision to perpetuate in his own family the temporal power which was his. At the first promulgation of his mission, the believers were a little

[1] Sura xlvii. 21.

knot of devoted friends, without power, but whose ardent faith and attachment were all in all to him, and provided him a more than sufficient recompense for the scorn and obloquy which he had to endure. Thus for many years he persevered, preaching and believing in the truth of his mission, never wavering in his faith, never doubtful of the reality of that revelation which called down upon him ridicule and persecution, which compelled some of his nearest relatives and followers to take refuge beyond the sea, which placed his life in danger, broke up his home, and, as a hunted fugitive drove him at last to take refuge in exile and in flight. Thus, then, in the absence of any more adequate reason, we are led to consider that a substantial belief in the reality of a divine commission to preach, and to re-establish in the world what he considered the original simple faith, sustained and impelled him forward, excited the enthusiasm of his adherents, and was the secret motive which called into being those spiritual claims of which the results have been so memorable.

And, as time goes on, we shall also find how these impulses, which at first may have aimed at the light, become more and more tinged with the things of earth and the things of sense; how, by degrees, the forbearance of his early years is abandoned, and is succeeded by acts of vindictive revenge, by rapine and lust; and how still he makes bold in believing these revelations which, under the name of the Almighty, are invoked to justify his deeds; and thus, by the very deceitfulness of his heart, he comes to consider his wild and sinful impulse as the will of Heaven, and as indubitable inspiration from on high.

CHAPTER IV.

MAHOMET'S LEGATION AND THE FIRST ESTABLISHMENT OF ISLAM.—[A.D. 610–617.]

WITH such religious speculations possessing his mind, he approached his fortieth year,[1] and was spending the month of Ramadhan in the cave of Hira. It was the night of Al Kadr, "which is better than a thousand months: therein do the angels descend, and the spirit of Gabriel also, by the permission of the Lord, with the decrees concerning every matter, and it is peace until the rising of the morn" (Koran, sura xcvii.),—when there appeared to him "one mighty in power, endued with understanding; . . . . he appeared in the highest part of the horizon. Afterwards, he approached the prophet, and drew near unto him, until he was at the distance of two bows' length from him, or yet nearer; and he revealed unto his servant that which he revealed" (Koran, sura liii.). It was the angel Gabriel, who held in his hand a silken cloth covered with writing, and bid Mahomet read; but he replied,

[1] Conf. Koran, sura x. 17:—"I have already dwelt among you [the men of Mecca] to the age of forty years."

that he could not. Then the angel, repeating part of the ninety-sixth sura, spoke as follows:—"Read in the name of the Lord, who hath created all things. Read, by the most beneficent Lord, who taught the use of the pen; who teacheth man that which he knoweth not" (Koran, sura xcvi. 1–5). And then the angel left him, and the words were as though they were engraved on his heart.[1] Such was the first appearance to him of the heavenly messenger, and the first intimation of the Divine will.

And then we are told that there was an interval of doubt and despondency in his mind; he was perplexed, and dreaded lest these beginnings of his inspiration might in reality be promptings of evil spirits and genii; and, driven to desperation, he contemplated suicide, but was held back by invisible hands. After a sufficient "intermission," the voice returned, and the angel, from a throne between heaven and earth, thus addressed him:—"Oh, Mohammed! thou art the apostle of God, and I am Gabriel." This intimation strengthened his heart, allayed his fears, and at length, persuaded of his divine appointment, he went to announce the glad tidings to Khadija.

Overjoyed at the news, she now understands the meaning of the strange visitations which had fallen on her husband, at once accepts the truth of his divine mission, and her faith, we learn, comforted and reassured him. Waraca, too, confirms the agitated mind of the prophet, and tells him that the

[1] Koran, sura ii. 91: "For he hath caused the Koran to descend on thy heart by the permission of God . . . a direction and good tidings to the faithful."

angel who had appeared to him was the same as announced to Moses his mission. Zeid, his adopted son, embraces the faith, and to these were added the names of two others, his adopted son Ali, and Abu Bekr, both afterwards caliphs, and both reckoned amongst the earliest believers. Ali was the son of Abu Talib, and cousin of the prophet, but nearly thirty years his junior. Abu Talib, however, had fallen on evil days, and when the burden of a numerous family pressed too heavily upon him, his former kindness to Mahomet was gratefully remembered, who, being then in affluent circumstances, took upon himself the charge of Ali, adopted him in place of his own lost Casim, and they afterwards felt towards each other the mutual attachment of parent and child. At the time when Mahomet assumed the prophetic character, Ali was about fourteen years of age, but with the permission of Abu Talib grew up in the faith of his adopted father.

Abu Bekr belonged to a collateral branch of the house of Coreish, being descended from Taym, the son of Morrah, the grandfather of the celebrated Cussai. He was about the same age, and the bosom friend of Mahomet; his charity was unbounded, his character gentle and unimpulsive, his passions always under the control of reason, and his firm and unwavering mind manifested no hesitation at the prophet's call to accept Islam. His proper name was Abdallah, and his firm attachment to Mahomet gained him the name of "Al-Sadiq," or "The True." In history he is celebrated under the name of Abu Bekr, or "the Father of the Virgin," a surname gained from the fact that Ayesha, his daughter, was the only virgin bride of the prophet.

By the influence of Abu Bekr five new converts were added to Islam: Saad, a nephew of Amina; Zobier, a nephew of Khadija; Talha, afterwards a valiant warrior of the faith; Othman-ibn-Affan,[1] subsequently caliph; and Abd-al-Rahman, the son of Awf, whose four companions, on their first visit to the prophet, embraced the new doctrines. Others were gradually added to the little band of the faithful. Of these may be mentioned Said-ibn-Zeid, then a boy, and his wife Fatima, sister of Zeid-ibn-Khattab, and of the famous Omar, afterwards caliph. In all, it may be assumed that in the first three or four years a small group of thirty or forty converts were the fruits of the secret preaching and private solicitation of the prophet.[2]

It was towards the end of this period that the prophet received, as he supposed, the divine command *to preach openly* the doctrines he had hitherto secretly promulgated. It was either on Mount Hira, or when, after being "reviled by certain of the Coreish, he was sitting pensive and wrapped in his mantle,"[3] that the same angelic messenger came, and thus addressed him:—"O thou covered, arise and preach, and magnify the Lord, and clean thy garments, and fly every abomination; and be not liberal in hopes to receive more in return, and patiently wait

[1] Othman was descended from Omeya, a son of Abd-Shams, and by his mother was a grandson of Abd-al-Muttalib.

[2] Muir, "Life of Mahomet," ii. 111, 112.

[3] Sale's "Koran," p. 471, note.

for thy Lord. . . . Let me alone with him [1] whom I have created, on whom I have bestowed abundant riches, . . . he is an adversary to our signs ; I will afflict him with grievous calamities. May he be cursed ; . . . and again may he be cursed ; . . . he was elated with pride ; and he said this is no other than a piece of magic, . . . I will cast him to be bound in hell" (Koran, sura lxxiv.).

Such then was the commission to preach openly, and as such it affords a view of the opposition which he had already met with, and of the form of that opposition. They taunted him with being a magician. We may also notice how, in his bitter and vindictive feelings, the authority of Heaven is sought to curse those who "frowned on him and put on an austere countenance, and turned their backs." [2] For, though

[1] The person alluded to is supposed to be Walid-ibn-al-Magheira, a chief man among the Coreish—the same who had begun the restoration of the Kaaba. Mahomet treats his uncle Abu-Lahâb with similar curses for the bitter hostility with which he sought to oppose the establishment of the new religion. Thus, "Let the hands of Abu-Lahâb perish (or let him be damned), and he shall perish. His riches shall not profit him . . . he shall go down to be burned into flaming fire ; and his wife also bearing wood, having on her neck a cord of twisted fibres of a palm-tree" (Koran, sura cxi.). Abu-Lahâb's wife, Om-Jemil, a sister of Abu-Sofian, had offended Mahomet by strewing thorns in his path, and thus comes in for her reward. Conf. Sale's "Koran," sura cxi. notes *ad loc.* ; Muir, ii. 80 ; Kasimirski, p. 538, note ; D'Herbelôt, art. "Abou-Lahab," who relates the traditional realization of Mahomet's curse.

[2] As a further specimen of this, the following may be mentioned. It is a quotation from the Koran, and is supposed to be levelled against Walid-ibn-al-Magheira : "Obey not any who is a common swearer, a despicable fellow, a defamer,

hitherto Mahomet had contented himself with making known his doctrines privately among his relatives and friends, and those whom their conversion allured to the new faith, the progress of his work had been sufficient to excite the hatred and alarm of the Coreish —the priestly caste—from whose ranks converts had been made, and to arouse the opposition of all those who directly or indirectly were interested in the conservation of the rites of the Kaaba, and the continuance of Mecca as a place of pilgrimage for the whole of Arabia.

We may be well assured that the chiefs of the Coreish were deeply interested in the retention of that idolatry which made Mecca at once a centre of religious resort and a flourishing and important commercial emporium. To attack its idols was to attack Mecca; for any diminution of the superstitious veneration in which it was held, would be followed by a loss of those pecuniary advantages which they derived from their sacerdotal functions, or their trade; and so it is found that while calling upon him for some heaven-sent proof[1] of the truth of the claims he

going about to slander . . . cruel . . . and besides this, of spurious birth . . . we will stigmatize him on the nose" (Sura lxviii. 11–16). Tradition says that the prophetical menace was made good at the battle of Bedr, where Walid had his nose slit! To reprove "common swearing," and condemn "slander" and "cruelty," is legitimate enough; but to reproach any man with his "spurious birth" betrays a degree of personal rancour altogether unworthy of the prophetic character to which he pretended. Yet the above are words put into the mouth of the Almighty!

[1] They demanded some miracle, such as turning the little hill Safâ into gold, &c.; but he refused, declared his inability, and

made, the partisans of the old faith subjected both Mahomet and his followers to scorn and ridicule, to insult and persecution. For, in order to accomplish their ends and arouse opposition, it was necessary only to raise the cry of impiety and disbelief in the national idols. In the earlier part of his career, the outrages of the excited populace were not confined to menaces alone, and on a certain occasion one of the assailants was wounded by Saad, who thus had the honour of shedding the first blood in the cause of Islam.

At the termination of the fifth year of his mission, Mahomet took up his abode in "the House of Arcam," which lay facing the Kaaba to the east; and there he received those who resorted to him for instruction in the principles of his belief, and for reading those portions of the Koran then revealed. From the important conversions there made it was afterwards styled "the House of Islam." Among the disciples here gained was a Christian slave named Jabr, from whom his enemies said he gained information regarding the Scriptures; and Suheib, a native of Mosul, in Mesopotamia, who had been made a captive, and sold a slave to Constantinople, and there educated and brought up. He came next to Mecca, where he gained his freedom and embraced Islam. He is supposed, on fair grounds, to be the person accused by his enemies as having furnished Mahomet with his Scriptural knowledge, and as thus alluded to: "Say, the holy spirit hath brought the Koran down from the Lord with truth, that

said that the power of working miracles belonged to God alone. Conf. sura vi. 109–111.

he may confirm those who believe. We, also, know that they say, Verily a certain man teacheth him to compose the Koran; the tongue of the person unto whom they incline is a foreign tongue," &c.[1] This person was deeply attached to Mahomet and his doctrine, and on his "flight," abandoning all his wealth, followed him to Medina.

And so believers were added till they reached about fifty; among whom are numbered many who were in menial or servile positions at Mecca. The incarcerations and tortures, chiefly by thirst in the burning rays of the sun, to which these humble converts were subjected, to induce their recantation and adoration of the national idols, touched the heart of Mahomet, and by divine authority he permitted them, under certain circumstances, to deny their faith, so long as their hearts were steadfast in it. Thus: "Whoever denieth God, after he hath believed, except him who shall be compelled against his will, whose heart continueth steadfast in the faith, shall be chastised" (Koran, sura xvi. 108).[2] It should be related that the history of Islam can afford examples of those who have refused to avail themselves of the permission here given, a permission which must be confessed to be subversive of all morality.[3]

Among the chief opponents of Mahomet and his doctrines were, as mentioned above, Walid and Abu Lahâb, his uncle; to these may be added Abu

[1] Koran, sura xvi. 104, 105.

[2] Conf. Sale, chap. xvi. p. 224.

[3] Conf. also 2 Kings v. 18, where the heathen Naaman asks forgiveness for "bowing in the house of Rimmon."

Sofian, the son of Harb, the grandson of Omeya, and great-grandson of Abd Shams. He was a man of great wealth, and one of the most influential men in Mecca. Abu Jahl,[1] a Coreishite, descended from Yokdha, uncle of Cussai was also a bitter and abusive opponent of the new doctrines. One day, having covered Mahomet, whom he met on the hill of Safa, with a shower of opprobrious epithets, and perhaps even blows—all which were patiently borne—the matter was reported to Hamza, Mahomet's uncle, a mighty hunter, who, with his bow and arrows, was just returning from the chase. Indignant, he pursued Abu Jahl, found him sitting in the Kaaba, inflicted immediate chastisement, and at once adopting

[1] Abu Jahl. The real name of this man, an implacable adversary of Mahomet, was Amru ibn Hestam, but was subsequently surnamed Abu Jahl, or the "Father of Folly." In the Koran he is thought to be alluded to thus :—"There is a man who disputeth concerning God, without either knowledge or a direction—proudly turning his side—on the resurrection we will make him taste the torment of burning" (Koran, sura xxii. 8, 9). His injustice to an orphan is also supposed to be alluded to in Sura cvii. 2, though the passage is also applied to Abu Sofian and to Walid ibn al Magheira. He advised the Meccans to put Mahomet to death. Thus : "Call to mind how the unbelievers plotted against thee, to put thee to death or expel thee the city, but God laid a plot against them; and God is the best layer of plots" (Koran, sura viii. 30 *et seq.*). He was a boastful, debauched man, and perished at the battle of Bedr. It is related of him that, being a near neighbour of Mahomet, he used to fling unclean and offensive things at the prophet and upon the hearth as he cooked his food. His example, it is added, was followed by some of the neighbours; but beyond such treatment and invective, Mahomet had to suffer hardly any injury of a personal nature.

the doctrines and faith of his nephew, was his faithful and vigorous supporter till his death at the battle of Ohod.

Up to the fifth year of his ministry (A.D. 615) Mahomet was probably free from the apprehension of personal danger, and in this he fared better than those converts of servile position, who were, as we have seen, exposed to chains and imprisonment, and whose scars and wounds showed the sufferings they had been called on to endure. His steady and constant protector was the amiable and venerable Abu Talib, who, though poor, yet, as the head of the house of Hashim, had both the power and inclination to shield from his hostile kinsmen the nephew who had been intrusted to his care, and yet whose faith he had not adopted.

It will perhaps be well at this stage to glance at the internal relations of Mahomet's family. As above related, his son Casim died at the age of two years. His eldest daughter, Zeinab, had been given in marriage to a Coreishite of the house of Abd-Shams, Abul-Aas by name, who was also a nephew, by his mother, of Khadija. On Mahomet's flight to Medina, she remained behind at Mecca with her husband, to whom she was much attached. The latter resisted the solicitations of his relatives to repudiate his wife. At the battle of Bedr, in which he fought against Mahomet, for he was not then a believer, he was taken prisoner and liberated on condition of sending Zeinab to her father. She died in the ninth year of the Hejira of the injuries she had received at the hands of the Coreish on her escape from Mecca; but before her death her husband had become a convert, and lived for a short time in happiness with her at Medina.

Rockeya and Omm Colthum, his second and third daughters, were married to Otba and Oteiba, sons of Abu Lahâb. On the assumption of the prophetic office, the latter, as we have seen, became one of Mahomet's bitterest opponents, and influenced his sons to repudiate their wives. Rockeya was then given to Othman-ibn-Affan. She was, as we shall see, with her husband, one of the emigrants to Abyssinia, and died ten or twelve years after her second marriage at Medina. Omm Colthum, repudiated as above mentioned, was, on the death of Rockeya, also united to Othman-ibn-Affan. She died before Zeinab. Fatima, between whom and Ali an attachment had gradually sprung up, was left behind at Mecca on Mahomet's flight, but joined him afterwards at Medina, and was married to her betrothed. Within two years she gave birth successively to two sons, Hasan and Hosein, who were born in the years A.D. 625 and 626.

To avoid the indignities and persecution to which many of his followers were exposed, Mahomet advised them to seek protection in a foreign land. The suggestion was adopted, and in the fifth year of his mission, eleven men, four of them with their wives, embarked at Shueiba, a port near Jiddah, and found a welcome asylum at the court of Abyssinia. Three months afterwards the fugitives returned, having received a report of the conversion of the Coreish to the new doctrines. This proving, without foundation, a second emigration took place about the year A.D. 616. Small bodies of converts from time to time joined themselves to the little band in Abyssinia, till their number amounted to about one hundred. Some returned afterwards to Mecca, and the rest joined Mahomet at Medina, in the seventh year of the Hejira.

The report which had reached the fugitives concerning the conversion of the Coreish arose from the following circumstance. It is said that at the time of their first departure a season of deep depression fell upon Mahomet. For years he had suffered the scorn and malice of his opponents; he had preached and prayed, and yet but fifty converts had been the fruits of his five years' mission. Barren as had been the results of the past, in the future he had before him a dark, cheerless prospect of continued opposition, of contumely, and perhaps of eventual failure. His heart and soul were wearied with waiting, and he longed, if it were possible, for a reconciliation. One day, whilst sitting by the Kaaba, he uttered, in the hearing of his opponents, words of compromise regarding their gods Al-Lât and Al-Ozza and Manah that "their intercession might be hoped for with God." These words were listened to with surprise by the idolaters who were present, and a reconciliation seemed possible; but within a few days the concession he had made was by the prophet attributed to a suggestion of the Evil One, was uncompromisingly withdrawn, and the idol-worship condemned and reprobated, thus:—"What think ye of Al-Lât, and Al-Ozza, and Manah, that other third goddess? . . . . they are no other than empty names, which ye and your fathers have named goddesses" (Sura liii. 19—23).

And, again:—"What think ye? Show me what part of the earth the idols which ye invoke, besides God, have created? Bring me a book of Scripture revealed before this, or some footstep of ancient knowledge, to countenance your idolatrous practices; if ye be men of veracity" (sura xlvi. 14, 15), where he asserts that no system of Scriptural belief ever countenanced idol-worship.

The trumpet of the prophet having given thus no uncertain sound, his ships were burnt on the strand, and the door of any compromise with the idolaters shut for ever. That he had strangely vacillated he long remembered, and felt often afterwards a deep consciousness of the danger he had run. In one of the later Meccan suras he thus writes:—"It wanted little, but the unbelievers had tempted thee to swerve from the instructions which we had revealed unto thee, that thou shouldst devise concerning us a different thing; and then would they have taken thee for their friend; and unless we had confirmed thee, thou hadst certainly been very near inclining unto them a little" (Koran, sura xviii. 75, 76).[1]

Doubtless this circumstance did him and his cause harm, gave his enemics a handle to reproach him with want of consistency, to call him a "Fabricator" and a "Forger,"[2] and induced them to assume an attitude of more decided hostility to him than before. Finding that Mahomet was not to be alarmed,

[1] On this see Sale's note *ad loc.*

[2] Suras xlvi. 6, 7; xvi. 103.

or brought to change his proceedings, they made an attempt to alienate from him the powerful and steady protection of his uncle, Abu Talib; and for this purpose sent to him a deputation of the most powerful and violent opponents of Islam. They represented to Abu Talib, who was still an adherent of the old superstition, that his nephew had spoken opprobriously of their idols, "saying that they be no gods which are made with hands," and had condemned their religion; moreover, that he had abused them as fools, and also given out that their forefathers had all gone astray;[1] and they requested that Mahomet might be left to them to be dealt with.

Abu Talib, with courteous and gentle words, refused to accede to their request, but representing matters firmly to his nephew, besought him that he would not lay on him a burden greater than he could bear. Mahomet was moved to tears by what he thought might end in his being abandoned by his guardian and protector, yet protested that neither the sun, nor the moon, nor death itself, could force him from his undertaking without the permission of God. Won by his courage and determination, Abu Talib bid him depart in peace, with the assurance that he would not abandon him for ever.[2]

The circumstances of the conversion of Hamza, called, from his heroism, the "Lion of God," have been related above. It was about this time (A.D. 616) that there was added to the faith a man who plays a distinguished part in the history of Islam—Omar-ibn-Al-Khattab—afterwards the second

[1] Muir, ii. 162.
[2] Id. ii. 168; W. Irving, p. 45.

Caliph, whose gigantic stature, prodigious strength, and valiant courage rendered him a fit companion to Hamza. He was at the time twenty-six years of age, was a Coreishite, descended from Ada—a brother of Morrah, and notorious for his enmity to the new faith. Aroused by the castigation which his near relative Abu Jahl had received at the hands of Hamza, he set out to seek revenge; but on the way it was hinted to him that his own sister—Fatima—had not escaped the taint of conversion. To her house, therefore, he went, and at the door overheard her and her husband reading the Koran.[1] Springing in, he wounded his sister in the face, but was induced to listen to the words they had been reading, on learning that the prophet had been praying for him, and for his conversion to the faith of those whom he had hitherto treated with such violence. The part of the Koran was as follows:—"We have not sent down the Koran unto thee that thou shouldst be unhappy; but for an admonition unto him who feareth God; being sent down from Him who created the earth and the lofty heavens. The Merciful sitteth on his throne; unto Him belongeth whatsoever is in heaven and on earth, and whatsoever is between them, and whatsoever is under the earth. If thou pronounce thy prayer with a loud voice, know that it is not necessary in respect to God; for He knoweth that which is secret, and what is yet more hidden. God! there is no God but He; He hath most excellent names" (Sura xx. 1–7).

[1] This fact proves that copies of the Suras were in use for private reading and devotion.

The words sank deep into his heart, and, in true keeping with his impulsive nature, he without hesitation went to the "house of Arcam," obtained admission, made the confession of faith, and was added to the number of believers. The adhesion of such men greatly strengthened Mahomet's position; "no one dared to approach or molest the Prophet, being deterred by the looks of those terrible men of battle Hamza and Omar, who, it is said, glared upon their enemies like two lions that had been robbed of their young."[1] We also read that "the Moslems no longer concealed their worship within their own dwellings, but with conscious strength and defiant attitude assembled in companies about the Kaaba, performed their rites of prayer, and compassed the holy house," while "dread and uneasiness seized the Coreish."[2]

Now that the followers of Mahomet had no longer need secretly to profess and practise their religion, converts of social power and influence were from time to time added to their number. But the hostile chiefs of the Coreish were not idle, and soon entered into a solemn confederacy to place a social and civil ban upon the new sect. The terms of this league were that they would neither intermarry with the proscribed, nor sell to or buy from them anything, and that they would entirely cease from all intercourse with them. Heavily, indeed, did this ostracism weigh upon those who fell under it. To avoid personal violence, they withdrew (A.D. 617) to

[1] W. Irving, p. 49. [2] Muir, ii. 172.

what is called the Sheb or quarter of Abu Talib, a secluded part of Mecca, lying under the rocks of the Abu Cobeis. A low gateway cut them off from the outer world, and within they had to suffer all the privations of a beleaguered garrison. No one could venture forth except in the sacred months, when all hostile feelings and acts had to be laid aside. Supplies at other times were with difficulty obtained, could be purchased, indeed, only from the foreign traders, and at exorbitant prices. "The citizens could hear the voices of the half-famished children inside the Sheb";[1] and this state of endurance on the one side, and persecution on the other, went on for some three years. Mahomet, in the intervals of the holy months, went forth and mingled with the pilgrims to Mecca, and at the annual fairs sought to propagate among them the especial doctrines of his sect, the abhorrence of idolatry, and the worship of the one true God. But few heeded him: they taunted him with the disbelief of his own kindred and townsfolk, and so, disheartened, but not dismayed, he returned to those devoted few, by whose faith he was comforted, and among whom he sought strength from God. Shut up thus with his disciples, whose hearts and affections he had won, and whose belief was confirmed by his own patient endurance and faith, we may now consider what was the nature of those doctrines, and of that teaching which could so firmly knit to himself the devotion of his loyal followers.

[1] Muir, ii. 175.

CHAPTER V.

EARLY TEACHING AT MECCA.—[A.D. 610–617.]

THE Koran, or inspired book of the Moslems, consists of one hundred and fourteen chapters or Suras, which vary much in length, some containing only a few lines, whilst the longest (the second) has as many as two hundred and eighty-six verses. It is made up of those revelations which Mahomet professed from time to time to have received direct from God, which he repeated to those about him, and of which, according to strict Mahometan doctrine, every word is of divine command. It is also by the Moslems considered the fountain head of all science, of all knowledge, and of all law. When made known, the different chapters, or parts of chapters—for it was seldom that an entire one was revealed at once—were by his followers committed to memory, or written down on palm-leaves, white stones, pieces of leather, shoulder-blades of the sheep and camel; and these in later years were put into a chest in the prophet's house, and subsequently came into the keeping of Haphsa, one of his wives. Copies of the suras, as they appeared, were, it seems, made for the private devotions of his followers. No complete copy of the several revelations which make up the present Koran appears to have existed during the lifetime of Mahomet; but during the caliphate of Abu Bekr, his successor, and at the suggestion of Omar, a copy was written out by the prophet's secretary, Zeid-ibn-Thâbit.

This was doubtless found an easy task, for having been in daily religious use, the different chapters were indelibly impressed on the accurate and retentive memory of the faithful. Indeed, a knowledge of the Koran in those early days, in addition to its being fraught with spiritual blessings, was considered the highest title to nobility: and certain of the prophet's contemporaries, as is the case at the present day, were able to repeat the whole book by heart. The copy made by Zeid was retained by Omar during his caliphate, and by him made over to his successor Othman. During his reign it was discovered that differences of reading had gradually crept into many of the copies made from Zeid's edition. These were all called in by the Caliph, a careful recension made, copies sent to the chief cities of the empire, and the incorrect manuscripts destroyed. Unfortunately the sequence of the chapters in the Koran, though asserted to be that prescribed by the prophet, does not follow the chronological order in which they were given, and is devoid of any intelligible arrangement, the revelations promulgated at Mecca before the Hejira, and afterwards at Medina, being thrown together apparently in the most careless and perplexing manner.[1] Yet there are ample and sufficient

[1] In Rodwell's "Translation of the Koran," the chronological order in which they are thought to have been revealed is preserved.

grounds for believing that the existing Koran consists of the genuine words, and is the original composition of the prophet, as learned or transcribed under his own instruction (Muir, i. c. sec. 1).

The whole of the Koran, therefore, as most probably the original delivered by the lips of Mahomet, forms a clear index to his own feelings, and ought to give an insight into the varying influence of external circumstances, were it found possible to arrange approximately the different chapters in the order and at the particular times when they were published. As it is, the chronological sequence of the different suras is to be gathered alone from the subject matter, and from clear references to passing events which may be discovered in them. Those which are considered the earliest are also the shortest, and are distinguished by their "wild and rhapsodical language, the counterpart of his internal struggles after the truth."[1] For it would seem that the religious emotions of Mahomet, and his early speculations unburdened themselves in strains of impassioned poetry; and of these fugitive pieces many which his followers had committed to memory afterwards found their way into the Koran.[2]

Eighteen of the chapters are assigned to that period of his career when, though he believed himself moved by a higher power to warn and admonish,

[1] Muir, ii. 58.

[2] For an account of the exegesis of the Koran, according to their modern divines, the reader should consult "Notes on Muhammadanism," by the Rev. T. P. Hughes (N. Quran), p. 11, *et seq.*

he had not received that direct commission to "preach openly," of which mention has already been made.

Of the eighteen [1] suras of this early period, the following extracts are specimens :—

Chapter ciii., entitled "The Afternoon." "In the name of the most merciful God.[2] By the afternoon; verily, man employeth himself in that which will prove of loss: except those who believe, and do that which is right, and who mutually recommend the truth, and mutually recommend perseverance unto each other" (conf. Psalm xxxix. 6).

Chapter c., entitled "The War-horses which run swiftly." This chapter is cast in a highly poetic strain; it invokes the war-horses which run swiftly and pant to the battle, whose hoofs strike fire and surprise the enemy in the early dawn, to bear witness that "man is ungrateful to his Lord"; but that the hidden thoughts of men's hearts will be brought to light, and that when the graves give up their dead, God will be fully informed concerning them (conf. Eccles. xii. 13, 14).

Chapter i., entitled "The Preface or Introduction." "Praise be to God, the Lord of all creatures; the most merciful, the King of the day of Judgment. Thee do we worship, and of Thee do we beg assistance. Direct us in the right way, in the

[1] The eighteen suras are numbered in the Koran as under :—103, 100, 99, 91, 106, 1, 101, 92, 102, 104, 82, 92, 105, 89, 90 93, 94, 108. (Muir, ii. Appendix.)

[2] All the suras except the 9th—the last revealed—begin with this invocation.

way of those to whom Thou hast been gracious; not of those against whom Thou art incensed,[1] nor of those who go astray." This chapter, which is here given in full, bears the title of "Al Fatihat," or the beginning; and is also called "The Seven Verses," "The Mother of the Book," and is held in great veneration by the Mahometans, and regularly repeated in their public and private devotions. It is a prayer for the guidance of God, and is directed to be repeated frequently (conf. Sura xv. 87).

Chapter xcix., entitled "The Earthquake," teaches the doctrine that God at the last day will reward men according to the deeds they have done; and this is insisted on in various other parts of the Koran. Thus: "Verily, if any do a good action God will recompense it in His sight with a great reward" (conf. Sura iv.). Again, "Verily, whoso doeth evil, and is compassed with his iniquities, they shall be companions of hell fire" (Sura ii. 75). Yet, it must be observed, that Mahomet has also declared that no person's good works will be sufficient to gain him admittance to Paradise, and that he himself would be saved, not by his merits, but by the mercy of God.

Chapter ci., entitled "The Striking." This is a powerful and vivid picture of the last day, and is so called because it will strike the hearts of all creatures with terror. "In that day we shall

[1] Supposed to allude to the Jews and Christians. As a rule, Mahomet speaks of the Christians much more tenderly than of the Jews; and we shall find that this feeling very much regulated his conduct towards the two.

be like moths scattered abroad, and the mountains shall become like carded wool of various colours driven by the wind. Moreover, he whose balance shall be heavy with good works shall lead a pleasing life; but as to him whose balance shall be light, his dwelling shall be in the pit of hell. It is a burning fire."

Chapter xcv. speaks of the original purity, the innocence, and the fall of man, and the vile condition of all, "Except those who believe and work righteousness, for they shall receive an endless reward. What, therefore, shall cause thee to deny the day of judgment after this? Is not God the most wise Judge?"

Chapter cii. reproves those emulously desirous of multiplying riches and children till they visit the grave. Tells them that hereafter their folly will be made manifest in hell (Sura xii. 13–21).

Chapter civ. "Woe to every slanderer and backbiter who heapeth up riches, and thinketh they can render him immortal. He shall be cast into 'Al Hotama,' the fire of hell kindled by God."

Chapter lxxxii., entitled "The Cleaving in sunder,"[1] refers to the last judgment. "When the heaven shall be cloven asunder; and when the stars shall be scattered;[2] and when the seas shall be suffered to join their waters; and when the graves [3] shall be turned upside down; every soul shall know what it hath committed, and what it hath omitted. O man! what hath seduced thee against thy gracious Lord, who hath created thee,

[1] 2 Peter iii. 10. [2] St. Matt. xxiv. 29.
[3] St. John v. 28, 29; Eccles. xii. 13, 14.

and put thee together, and rightly disposed thee? In what form He pleased hath He fashioned thee.[1] Assuredly. But ye deny the last judgment as a falsehood. Verily, there are appointed over you guardian angels, honourable in the sight of God, writing down your actions,[2] who know that which you do. The just shall surely be in a place of delight; but the wicked shall surely be in hell; they shall be cast therein to be burned on the day of judgment, and they shall not be absent therefrom for ever.[3] What shall cause thee to understand what the day of judgment is? It is a day on which one soul shall not be able to obtain anything on behalf of another soul; and the command on that day shall be God's." The reader will notice, from the references in the note below, how Scriptural much of the above is. The statement in the concluding paragraph, that "one soul shall not be able to obtain anything on behalf of another soul," is consistently sustained throughout the Koran, and amounts to a direct denial of the Redemption.

Chapter cv. is a short song of victory, on the defeat of Abraha, who, in the year of Mahomet's birth, advanced towards Mecca to destroy the Kaaba. It is entitled "The Elephant," from the animal upon which Abraha rode; and is quoted here at length, as perhaps the earliest specimen of the way in which fabulous traditional stories are introduced into the Koran, with the supposed authority of inspiration:—

[1] Ps. cxix. 73, and cxxxix. 16; Romans ix. 20.

[2] Gen. xlviii. 16; Ps. xci. 11, 12, and lvi. 8; St. Matt. xviii. 10; Phil. iv. 3; Rev. iii. 5; xiii. 8; xx. 12, 13.

[3] Rev. xiv. 11.

"Hast thou not seen how thy Lord dealt with the masters of the elephant? Did He not make their treacherous design an occasion of drawing them into error; and send against them flocks of birds, which cast down upon them stones of baked clay; and rendered them like the leaves of corn eaten by cattle?" The commentators say that flocks of birds, like swallows, pursued the retreating host, and destroyed it in the manner related above. They also assert that on each stone was written the name of its intended victim! The Koran, itself, gives a similar account of the way in which the inhabitants of Sodom were destroyed (Sura xv. 74):—"We turned those cities upside down, and we rained upon them stones of baked clay, one following another, and being marked."

Chapter xc., entitled "The Territory," tells that there are two highways—the path of good and the path of evil. The former is likened to a cliff, of which the ascent is difficult; for "it is to free the captive, or to feed in the day of famine the orphan who is of kin, or the poor man who lieth on the ground." They who do this "shall be the companions of the right hand," "but they who shall disbelieve in our signs shall be the companions of the left hand, and over them shall be arched fire."

In Chapter xciii., he comforts his heart with a remembrance of the goodness and mercy which have followed him. "By the brightness of the morning, and by the night when it groweth dark, thy Lord hath not forsaken thee, neither doth He hate thee. Verily, the life to come shall be better for thee than this present life; and thy Lord shall give thee a reward with which thou shalt be well pleased. Did He not find thee an orphan, and hath He not taken care of thee? And did He not find thee wandering in error, and hath He not guided thee into the truth?"

Such, then, is a somewhat detailed view of those "revelations" which he asserted to have come to him before he received the direct announcement of the angel Gabriel, that he was the chosen prophet of the Lord, and was directed to preach openly; and it will be admitted that, as far as they go, there is nothing in their morality to which we, as Christians, need take exception. In them we find him seeking direction from that gracious Lord, the God of all creatures, who knows the secrets of all hearts, and who, when the graves are opened, will bring to light every secret thing written in the book of His remembrance.

We meet with the statement that men will be judged according to the deeds done in the body at the last day, when the mountains shall be carried into the midst of the sea, and the earth shall be removed; and that the wicked shall go into everlasting punishment, but the righteous into everlasting happiness. We meet with the assertion of the original purity, and also of the fall of man, and that the most wise Judge will condemn all, except those who believe and work righteousness. Further, we have repeated warnings of the folly of those who trust in their riches to profit them, and to secure immortality. Against the slanderer and backbiter wrath and woe are denounced; the existence of two paths—of good and of evil—is pointed out; and the duty is insisted on of ministering to the captive, the orphan, and the dying, and also of shunning idolatry, and of giving alms. And, lastly, we have an acknowledgment of a righteous judgment to come; of God's power and overruling Providence, and a grateful mention of the goodness of the Almighty, who found him an orphan, and led him all his life long; who met him wandering in error, and guided him to the truth.

But not only do we find much to commend in these earlier suras, we also notice the absence of those personal feelings of revenge, which he afterwards allowed to burst forth in scathing invective, and for which he claims the high authority of Heaven. Up to this time, indeed, the time of his commission to preach openly, opposition had not grown fierce—the vital interests of personal profit and loss, family rights and phylarchical prerogatives were not yet at stake; even the gods of Mecca seemed hardly in danger, and had not begun to totter on their thrones. But now the change creeps in, the strife grows hot; disciples must be attracted to the new faith, and, once attracted, they must be retained. Now, therefore, the grosser elements of earth begin to mingle with the more spiritual utterances of an earlier time. Elaborate descriptions of the torments of hell, reserved for the wicked, the unjust, the covetous, and those who "charge the Koran with falsehood," deal terror to the unbeliever; while sensuous, pictures of the delights and rewards reserved for the "faithful," in his material heaven, promise fresh and unsatiating pleasures to those who believe.

The chapters revealed between his command to preach publicly and the time of the first Hejira, to Abyssinia, a period of two years, are reckoned at about twenty.[1] They are generally much longer than those we have been considering, and too long for entire quotation, or even for separate examination. I shall, therefore, seek to group them together, and to give such extracts from them as my space will allow, and as may best convey a general idea of their subject-matter.

In the chapters, then, of this second period, the doctrine of Predestination, or Fate, is inculcated (Sura lxxiv. 3, 4). "Thus doth God cause to err whom He pleaseth, and He directeth whom He pleaseth"; and again, in the same chapter (v. 54, 55), "Whoso is willing to be warned, him shall the Koran warn; but they shall not be warned unless God shall please." This doctrine appears also in Sura xcii. 4, where it is stated that on the night of Al Kadr "Gabriel descends with the Lord's decrees concerning every matter" regarding which the Mahometans believe that on that night the events of the ensuing year are fixed by God. This doctrine is further insisted upon in the chapters of a later date, and generally leavens their whole teaching. Thus (Sura xvii. 14), "The fate of every man have we bound round his neck"; and again (Sura iii. 139), "No soul can die unless

[1] A.D. 613–615. These suras are numbered thus:—96, 112, 74, 87, 97, 88, 80, 81, 84, 86, 110, 85, 63, 78, 77, 76, 75, 70, 109, 107, 55, 56.

by the permission of God, according to what is written in the book of the Determination of Things."[1]

Thus the Mahometans accept the doctrine of God's absolute predestinating decree, both for good and evil, for man's obedience and disobedience, for his future happiness and misery, and also that these eternal and immutable decrees cannot by any wisdom or foresight be avoided. Carried to its extreme, this doctrine saps the foundation of free-will, renders men blind to the teaching of the past, apathetic in the present, and indifferent to the future. It makes prayer an empty form, destroying as it does all dependence upon an overruling Providence, and, pitiless as the grave, takes away alike the power of avoiding sin, and of escaping its punishment; making even the power and mercy of the Almighty subject to the fiat of an inexorable Fate.

But it should be remarked that Mahomet was far from carrying this doctrine to that extreme length which it has reached in the opinions and practice of the great mass of his followers. He seems to have been deeply imbued with a belief in the power of an overruling Providence, and in the duty and efficacy of prayer, which, indeed, he says "preserves man from crimes, and from that which is blamable" (Sura xxix. 44). Take also the following passage:—"Follow the most excellent instructions which have

[1] "This revelation was obtained to still the murmurs and grief of those who lost relatives at the disastrous battle of Ohod (A.D. 625), where Mahomet was defeated. He assured them that, had those who fell in battle remained at home, they could not have avoided their fate, whereas they now had the advantage of dying martyrs for the faith."—SALE.

been sent down unto you from your Lord, before the punishment come suddenly upon you . . . and a man shall say, Alas ! for that I have been negligent in my duty to God ; verily I have been one of the scorners : or say, if God had directed me, verily I had been one of the pious : or say . . . if I could return once more into the world, I would become one of the righteous. But God shall answer, My signs came unto thee heretofore . . . and thou becamest one of the unbelievers." Here is clearly "free-will" preached. On such a mysterious subject, any teaching is naturally ambiguous, "and the doctrine has given rise to as much controversy among the Moslems as among Christians."[1]

In the chapters of this period is seen the first hint of that doctrine which he probably began to find both necessary and convenient; viz. that God had it in His power to annul or abrogate any revelation of the Koran once given, or to supply its place with a different one. "This doctrine offered an irresistible temptation to suit the substance of the Koran to the varying necessities of the hour."[2] Thus (Sura lxxxvii. 6, 7), "We will enable thee to rehearse our revelations, and thou shalt not forget any part thereof, *except what God shall please;* for He knoweth what is manifest and what is hidden." At a later period this power is more strongly insisted on (Sura ii. 100) : "Whatever verse we shall abrogate, or cause thee to forget, we shall bring a better than it, or one like unto it. Dost thou not know that God is Almighty ?"

[1] Lane, "Modern Egyptians," vol. i. p. 9.

[2] Muir, vol. ii. p. 157. See also "Notes on Muhammadanism," Hughes, p. 24, regarding these "abrogated passages."

It might be suggested here to a thoughtful Mahometan that this was a severe test to which the prophet's belief in his own inspiration was put, implying, as it did, that the revelations of an earlier date might prove defective, and even erroneous. Indeed, he seems to have felt this for his disciples, for we find that soon afterwards particular injunction is laid upon them not to waver in their loyalty to the "excellent Koran, the original whereof is written in the preserved book . . . a revelation from the Lord of all creatures."[1]

Hence some of the Mahometans deny that the Koran was the composition of their prophet, and assert that it is eternal, and uncreated, and of the essence of God Himself.[2] Others refuse to detract from the honour of God by making anything co-equal with or not created by Him; though they, too, are unanimous in their belief that Mahomet was merely the medium for conveying God's will to men, and that his words, therefore, are the words of the Almighty, who speaks in every sentence.

The Unitarian doctrine is asserted in the 112th Sura, which is as follows (title, "The Declaration of God's Unity"):—"In the name of the most merciful God. Say, God is one God, the eternal God: He begetteth not, neither is He begotten: and there is not any one like unto Him." This chapter

[1] See also Sura lxxxv. 21, 22.

[2] Conf. D'Herbelôt, art. "Alcoran," for details of the dispute on this subject. Motavakkel, the 10th caliph of the Abbassides (A.H. 231), published an edict allowing the faithful to believe what they liked in the matter.

is held in particular veneration by the Mahometans, and is declared by a tradition of their prophet to be equal in value to a third part of the whole Koran.[1]

The doctrine of the Unity of the Godhead, in contradistinction to the Christian belief in the Trinity in Unity, is continually insisted upon in the Koran, and may be said to be the characteristic tenet, the foundation-stone of the faith of Islam. This dogma, to which is added that of the belief in the mission of Mahomet, is ever in the mouth of the devout Moslem, the formula being, "THERE IS NO GOD BUT GOD, AND MAHOMET IS THE PROPHET OF GOD."

In later chapters the doctrine of the Unity of God is repeatedly insisted upon in refutation of the doctrine held, or supposed to be held, by the followers of other religions. Thus (Sura xxiii. 95) "God hath not begotten issue, neither is there any other God with Him." And again (Sura ii. 110), "They [the Jews and the Christians] say God hath begotten children: God forbid"! Again (Sura xvi. 59), "They [the idolaters] attribute daughters to God: far be it from Him." And again (Sura xxxvii. 146), "Do they [the people of Mecca] not say of their own false invention, God hath begotten issue: and are they not really liars?"

At this period we find him clearly renouncing the idolatry of the Kaaba. It is said that certain of the Coreish having proposed to him either to associate the worship of his God with that of their gods, or to worship them alternately for a year, he at once

[1] Sale.

rejected the compromise, and his refusal is contained in Sura cix., entitled "The Unbelievers." "In the name of the most merciful God."—"Say, O unbelievers, I will not worship that which ye worship; nor will ye worship that which I worship."

It is not to be supposed by this that Mahomet disapproved of the veneration given to the "holy places," which were hallowed in the traditions of their fathers, though disfigured by the later introduction of idolatry. It was against the latter only that he waged uncompromising war. It will be found hereafter that he upheld the ancient rites of the Kaaba, and established it as the Kibla, or Point of Adoration, towards which the Faithful were to turn.

At first, neither he nor his adherents appear to have followed in this respect any particular use, it being declared to be perfectly indifferent. Thus: "To God belongeth the east and the west; therefore whithersoever ye turn yourselves to pray, there is the face of God, for God is omnipresent and omniscient."

But afterwards, when the prophet fled to Medina, and, possibly with the hope of alluring the Jews of that place to his worship, he established "Jerusalem" as the place towards which they were to pray.[2]

This continued for some time, but failed in accomplishing the object Mahomet had in view. Afterwards, [3] to satisfy his own ardent wish, and the desire of his Arab followers, who were deeply attached to the national shrine, he made Mecca the Kibla towards

[1] Sura ii. 109.

[2] Conf. I Kings viii. 29, 44, 48; Ps. v. 7; Dan. vi. 10.

[3] About sixteen months after his arrival at Medina, A.D. 623.

which, in whatever part of the world they might be their prayers were to be directed. Thus,[1] "Turn therefore thy face towards the holy temple of Mecca, and wherever ye be, turn your faces towards that place." And later,[2] he received a further revelation on this head, asserting the antiquity of Mecca as a place of worship, and its being a Kibla for all nations. Thus:[3] "Verily, the first house appointed unto men to worship in was that which is in Becca;[4] blessed, and a direction to all creatures."

To this period also belong those outbursts of vituperation against those who opposed him, of which mention has already been made. How widely the spirit thus shown by Mahomet differs from that of our blessed Lord under like provocation, "who, when He was reviled, reviled not again"; and who, with love strong unto death, thus prayed for His murderers:—"Father, forgive them, for they know not what they do."

And yet these chapters contain an interesting proof of Mahomet's candour and magnanimity. The 80th Sura is entitled "He frowned," and in it he administers a rebuke to himself for having paid more respect and attention to some of the powerful Coreish, with whom he was in conversation, than to a poor blind man who came to him and asked to be taught about God. Thus:[5] "The Prophet frowned and turned aside, because the blind man came to him. . . . The man who is wealthy thou receivest respectfully; . . . but him who cometh unto thee earnestly seeking

[1] Sura ii. 139. [2] A.D. 624. [3] Sura iii. 90.
[4] Ancient name of Mecca. [5] Sura lxxx. 1–11.

salvation, and who feareth God, dost thou neglect. By no means shouldest thou act thus."

In the 70th chapter, God bids him "bear the insults" of the Meccans with becoming patience, "for they see their punishment afar off, but we see it nigh at hand."

Various other subjects are treated of at this time. The persecutions of the Christians of Najrân, whom he calls "true believers," by Dzu Nowâs, is reprobated:[1] the power and goodness of God are extolled "in causing corn to spring forth, and giving grapes, and clover, and the olive, and the palm, and gardens planted with thick trees, and fruits, and grass for the use of yourselves and your cattle."[2] Wrath is denounced against "those who give short measure or weight, and defraud";[3] and destruction and woe to those "who accused the Prophet of imposture."[4] The certainty of the resurrection is asserted, and we are told that on that day the wicked "will seek a place of refuge, and shall find none";[5] and that he "shall wish in vain to redeem himself from punishment, by giving up his children, and his wife, and his brother."[6] We are further told that "in that inevitable day" all men shall be separated into three classes, "the companions of the right hand, and the companions of the left hand; and those who have preceded others in the faith shall precede them in paradise."

In the 70th chapter is found the first official permission given to cohabitation, or concubinage with female slaves obtained by purchase, or made captive in

[1] Sura lxxiv. [2] Sura lxxv. [3] Sura lxx.
[4] Sura lxxvii. [5] Sura lxxv. [6] Sura lxx.

war (called "those whom your right hands possess"), in addition to their lawful wives.[1] The above permission "was one of the earliest compromises by which Mahomet fitted his system to the usages and wants of those about him; and was, in after days, largely taken advantage of, both for his own indulgence, and as holding out an inducement for his followers to fight in the hope of capturing females who would then be lawful concubines."[2]

To this period finally belong those gross pictures of heaven and hell, which, if accepted in their literal sense, are sufficient in themselves to disprove the claim made by their author to Divine inspiration. Doubtless, their material delights would prove irresistibly fascinating to the Arabs living in such a climate in such a scorched and desert land. The prospect of exchanging their toils amid the burning sands and naked rocks of Arabia for "long rest and dreamful ease" upon soft beds, in cool shaded gardens, beside murmuring waters, and tended by the beautiful black-eyed girls of Paradise, must have been ineffably attractive.

Hell is described in terms of a kindred colouring. Thus,[3] the wicked "shall be cast into scorching fire to be broiled: they shall be given to drink of a boiling fountain: they shall have no food, but of dry thorns and thistles." Again: "The companions of the left hand shall dwell amidst burning winds and scalding water, under the shade of a black smoke."[4]

[1] Sura lxv. 28–31; iv. 28.
[2] Muir, ii. 140, note.
[3] Sura lxxxviii. 3–6.
[4] Conf. Sura xxxvii. 62 66.

The joys of Heaven are thus depicted.[1] The just "shall drink of a cup of wine mixed with the water of Cafur,"[2] and shall be rewarded "with a garden and silk garments: therein shall they repose themselves on couches—fruits shall hang low" near them, "so as to be easily gathered." And they shall have besides "two other gardens"—"of a dark green"—"in each of them shall be two fountains of water"—"fruits and palm-trees, and agreeable and beauteous damsels"—"having fine black eyes; and kept in pavilions from public view."[3]

The sensuous delights of Mahomet's paradise are by some of his apologists accepted as allegorical pictures of more spiritual pleasures, and are not, they say, intended to be understood according to their literal sense.

True indeed it is, that in Holy Scripture God shows His condescension in the form which He allows Divine truth to take, using, as He does, human language, and imagery drawn from material objects, suited to the finite comprehension of His children. Thus veiled, we are enabled to gaze upon the light of heaven, and though softened and tempered to our weakness, it is still the unchanged Word of God. Thus the ecstatic vision in Patmos tells us of the pearly gates and golden streets of the New Jerusalem, of "the water of life," and the tree whose "leaves are

[1] Sura lxxvi. [2] Camphor.

[3] Sura lv. The Mahometans assert that there are seven heavens, or stages of celestial bliss in Paradise, and seven divisions of hell for the reception, respectively, of guilty Mahometans, Christians, Jews, Sabeans, Magi, Idolaters, and for Hypocrites.

for the healing of the nations": moreover, we read how, at the Last Supper, our blessed Lord spake of that "fruit of the vine" of which He would drink hereafter in the kingdom of His Father. But these humanized ideas of happiness contain no element of grossness or possible impurity, and are evidently to be interpreted by the light of those other passages, which point to the absence of all sin and grief, and the immediate presence of a holy God, as the highest bliss of the Christian heaven.

The Koran, indeed, teaches that there are differing degrees of happiness in heaven, and the reward of the most favoured seems associated with the beatific vision.[1] We read that there, among the believers, "there shall be no vain discourse," and "no incitement to wickedness,"[2] expressions which would imply a state of at least passive goodness. Yet how can we suppose that grosser joys and feelings are excluded, when we read that in Paradise the true believers, "lying on couches," "shall look down upon the infidels [in hell] and shall laugh them to scorn."[3] Such feelings surely could not find place in the hearts of beings who were freed from the dross and corruption of earth.

The truth seems to be, that Mahomet was unable to form any estimate of celestial happiness apart from the sensual indulgences, to which the story of his life shows him to have been so keenly addicted; and however much some of his followers may try to explain away his sensuous descriptions,

[1] Sura lxxxiii. 28. [2] Sura lii. 2.
[3] Sura lxxxiii. 34, 35.

"the general and orthodox doctrine is, that the whole is to be strictly believed in the obvious and literal acceptation."[1]

Another learned author, writing of the heaven of Mahomet, says: "It must be admitted that spiritual pleasures and the favour of God are also said to form part of its delights, and that the permanence of man's personality is implied. But a holy God is still immeasurably removed from His creatures, and intimate union with Him, or even admission to His presence, is not the central idea of beatitude."[2]

From a careful perusal of the suras of this second period, it may safely be said that there is nothing in them which an Arab, acquainted with the general outline of the Jewish history and legend, and of the traditions of his own country, and possessed of some poetic fire and fancy, might not have written, and that the hypothesis of a divine origin is in no way required to account for them.

The details of the history and doings of certain beings who are called Genii, repeatedly referred to in the Koran, may here be cited as a specimen of the curious working of Mahomet's mind. It is to be borne in mind that the statements regarding them are supposed to be made by Divine authority, and even to be the very words of God Himself.

These allusions to the Genii show that the belief in the existence of these spectral beings was one of

[1] Sale, P. D., p. 102.

[2] Monier Williams, "Indian Wisdom," Intr., p. xxxix.

a popular character in Arabia at the time of Mahomet, and that he probably drank in with his earliest experience the weird stories that associated Genii with the deserts and mountains of his native land.

Poetic fancy, indeed, in other climes has wandered in the same path and peopled the world with troops of impalpable beings; has given the dryad to the woods, the oread to the mountain heights; has conjured up fay and kelpie, satyr and fawn, and all the elfin crew; and, with superstitious dread of the unseen, has shaped the forms of wicked sprite, malicious demon, and hideous ghoul, to haunt the cities of the dead, and wreak on the living their hatred and revenge.[1]

When such fancies occur in fairy story they find their use; but when they are put forth as facts invested with Divine authority, the absurdity becomes apparent to intelligent minds.

This, then, is what the Koran says of these beings. They are represented as having been created by God of "subtle fire,"[2] for no other purpose than to serve Him.[3] They were believed by the old Arabians to haunt desert places, and to "protect those who fled to them for refuge," and, like the idolaters around them, to believe that there was no resurrection.[4] These words are put into the mouth of the Genii:—"And we formerly attempted to pry into what was

[1] For an exhaustive account of these beings [Jinn, &c.], *vide* Lane, "Arabian Nights," notes to the Introduction, vol. i. No. 21.

[2] Sura xv. 27.

[3] Sura li. 5, 6

[4] Sura lxxii. 6, 7.

transacting in heaven, but we found the same filled with a strong guard of angels, and with flaming darts; and we sat on some of the seats thereof to hear the discourse of its inhabitants; but whoever listeneth now, findeth a flame laid in ambush for him, to guard the celestial confines."—"And when we could not frustrate God, and had heard the Koran, we believed therein."—"Some of us are Moslems"—"and whoso embraceth Islam, they earnestly seek true direction."[1]

We are told that certain of the Genii, when the prophet was resting in the valley of Nakhla, during his escape from Tayif, overheard him reading the Koran, and believed; and they are represented as preaching to their fellows, and urging upon them "a belief in Mahomet, to escape a painful punishment."[2] The Koran is said to have been sent to save both men and Genii.

The shooting stars are, by the Moslems, believed to be heaven's artillery, used for the dispersion of the genii and devils, who listen to catch by stealth scraps of the celestial secrets, for the purpose of giving them, like the Promethean fire, to mortals.[3]

The Genii are stated to have been forced to work in Solomon's presence, "and they made him whatever he pleased"—"of palaces, and statues, and large dishes like fish-ponds":[4] and, finally, his army is said to have consisted of "genii, and men and birds."[5]

We now enter upon the consideration of the third

[1] Sura lxxii. 6–14.
[2] Sura xlvi. 30.
[3] Sura lxvii. 6.
[4] Sura xxxiv. 11, 12.
[5] *Vide* D'Herbelôt, art. "Ginn."

group of suras.[1] Here begin the more detailed references to the Jewish Scriptures, and the laborious arguments drawn from the rejection of God's prophets by the Jews, by which Mahomet sought to establish his own claims against the incredulous Meccans, of which we shall have more to say further on. Imaginary conversations are held here between the ancient people and those who were sent to them, and words are put into the mouths of the old Patriarchs and Prophets, so that they, like the Genii, are made to speak Mahomet's warnings, and express his thoughts, and to thus adroitly support the teaching which he had addressed to the idolatrous Meccans: and further, the very objections which these latter made to him are represented as being identical with those urged by the unbelievers in former ages, and which are shown to have brought down upon them the fiery vengeance of Heaven.

We gather from these suras that his opponents accused him of imposture;[2] called him "soothsayer";[3] denied him the title of "an honourable apostle";[4] stigmatized him as a "distracted poet," and his warnings as "manifest sorcery."[5] They ascribed the origin of the Koran to devils,[6] and teased him for a sign of the authenticity of his mission.[7]

As a specimen of the kind of argument used by Mahomet, I give the following:[8]—The chapter

[1] *Vide* Muir, II. Appendix. The twenty suras are numbered in the Koran as follows:—67, 53, 32, 39, 73, 79, 54, 34, 31, 69, 68, 41, 71, 52, 50, 45, 44, 37, 30, 26, 15, 51; A.D. 615–619.

[2] Sura lxxvii. *passim*; lii. 2, &c.

[3] Sura lxix. 41.

[4] Sura lxix. 40..

[5] Sura xxxvii. 15.

[6] Sura xxvi. 210.

[7] Sura xxvi. 187.

[8] Sura xv. 1–15.

[xv.] is entitled "Al Hajar," a territory in the Hejaz, between Medina and Syria, where the tribe of Thamud dwelt. They had fallen into idolatry, and therefore "the prophet Saleh was sent to bring them back to the worship of the true God"; but they rejected him, and, acting impiously, were destroyed by an earthquake. To this nation and its fate repeated reference is made in the Koran.[1] "These are the signs of the book and of the perspicuous Koran. The time may come when the unbelievers shall wish they had been Moslems." "We have not destroyed any city, but a fixed term of repentance was appointed them. No nation shall be punished before their time shall be come, neither shall they be respited after. The Meccans say, O thou to whom the admonition hath been sent down, thou art certainly possessed with a devil! Wouldest thou not have come unto us with an attendance of angels, if thou hadst spoken truth? Answer: We send not down angels unless on just occasion."—"We have sent apostles before thee among the ancient sects, and there came no apostle unto them, but they laughed him to scorn. In the self-same manner will we put it into the hearts of the wicked Meccans to scoff at their prophet."—"If we should open a gate in the heaven above them, and they should ascend thereto all the day long, they would surely say, Our eyes are only dazzled."

In this last sentence he makes the Almighty give His reason for *not* performing a miracle, to attest the validity of His servants' mission; and in the 26th sura we find Him consoling Mahomet under the same

[1] *Vide* Sale, P. D., p. 7. Sura xv. note, *ad loc.*

kind of reproach, and pointing out that the Meccans have continually before them the signs of His Almighty power, that He causes the fruits of "every noble species" to spring up, and that of old He has shown His wonders and judgments on those who turned away from Him, and that, if they accept not these, no special miracle would have any effect upon their stubborn and hardened minds.[1]

On this head it may be remarked that Mahomet always disclaimed the power of working miracles, and assumed no higher honour than that of being a prophet sent by God—"a warner," an apostle—the instrument of communicating God's will to men; and the honesty of his conduct in this respect speaks well for him, and implies a perfect reliance on the goodness of his cause.

To those who demanded from him some miraculous proof of the truth of his claims, he pointed to the Koran—a book revealed to "an ignorant and unlearned man,"[2] as the greatest of miracles, and he assured the objectors that if not convinced by it, no sign, however stupendous, would have power to compel their belief.[3]

During this period he claims for the Koran authority supplementary and superior to that of the "Book of the Law," which had been given to the people of Israel.[4] Thus, "We gave to the children

[1] Sura xxvi. 1–5. [2] Sura vii. 156.

[3] Compare Luke xvi. 31.

[4] Though the Mahometan doctors are driven to say that the Koran has abrogated the Old and New Testaments, there is no authority for the assertion in the teaching of the book itself. Thus: "Oh, children of Israel, believe in the revelation"

of Israel the Book of the Law, and wisdom, and prophecy, and we fed them with good things"; but they fell to "variance among themselves through envy"; afterwards, "we appointed thee, O Mohammed, to promulgate a law concerning the business of religion; wherefore follow the same." "This Koran is a direction and a mercy unto people who judge aright."[1]

Mention has already been made of the angel Gabriel, and his announcement to Mahomet that he was appointed the "prophet of God"; and as two other of these spiritual beings are alluded to in the chapters of this period, it may be well to consider what is the teaching of the Koran, and the belief of its followers regarding them. They are represented as having been created by God, and as partaking, like the Genii, of the nature of fire,[2] as capable of falling, but without the gross passions of the Genii. They are God's messengers to men,[3] and are of different grades.[4] They are appointed to bear God's throne aloft at the last day.[5] Two of them attend continually to the work of noting down the good and bad actions and words of each mortal;[7] and they are appointed to guard the celestial regions from the near approach of wicked spirits.

Of the angelic beings who surround the throne of God there are four of the highest dignity and power. *Gabriel*, the Angel of Revelation, who com-

(Koran) "which I have sent down, *confirming that which is with you*" (Sura ii. 38). Cf. "Notes on Muhammadanism," p. 25. See also sura v. 52.

[1] Sura xlv. 15–19.
[2] Sura vii. 11. Comp. Heb. i. 7.
[3] Sura xviii. 2.
[4] Sura xxxv. 1.
[5] Sura lxix. 17.
[6] Sura l. 16, 17.

municated the Koran to Mahomet,[1] and is said therein to have been sent by God to the Virgin Mary, to promise her "a Holy Son."[2] *Michael*, "the Friend of the Jews," mentioned in conjunction with Gabriel as one of those, enmity against whom involves enmity against God Himself.[3] *Azrael*, called "the Angel of Death," who separates men's souls and bodies,[4] and with his assistants either "tears them asunder with violence, or draws them apart with gentleness."[5] *Israfil*, whose business it will be to sound the two trumpets at the last day.[6]

The devil, named *Eblis* in the Koran, was once one of the archangels in heaven, and was called Azazil, but by disobedience fell, under circumstances thus related:—"And we created Adam, and said to the angels, worship Adam, and they all worshipped him except Eblis," who refused, and said, "I am more excellent than he: Thou hast created me of fire, and hast created him of clay";[7] for this God drove him down from Paradise, and, being respited till the day of judgment, his business is to "tempt man to disobedience on the earth," but he has no power over God's servants, but only over those "who shall be seduced."[8]

[1] Sura ii. 91. [2] Sura xix. 17–19.
[3] Sura ii. 92. [4] Sura xxxii. 2. [5] Sura lxxix. 1.
[6] Sura xxxix. 68. Compare 1 Thess. iv. 16.
[7] Sura vii. 9–11.
[8] Sura xv. 39–42. A recent writer forcibly points out the palpable contradiction of the Koran in the order given by God to Eblis to worship Adam thus:—"Satan's fall is represented as caused by his refusal to worship Adam at God's command when the other angels obeyed; that is, for refusing to render the creature the homage due to the Creator alone—a sin more

In all that the Koran teaches on this head we find no parallel to that comforting belief in the "ministry of angels," which the Christian gathers from the few transient glimpses into the mystery of God's kingdom, afforded by the New Testament regarding the employments of these pure intelligences. They sang, as we remember, to the astonished shepherds their heavenly songs of gratulation on the birth of the Saviour. Their ministry it was which the Son of Man deigned to accept when, wearied with fasting, He had foiled the tempter; and, again, in the fearful hour of the agony in the garden, He was willing to take comfort from those whom He had made—the Creator from the creature. We are told that these happy beings—an innumerable company—stand around the throne of God, and that they rejoice over "every sinner that repenteth"; that the "angels" of those "little ones," whom the Saviour loves, stand ever in the presence of the Father and behold His face. We are also told that the angels "desire to look into" the great mysteries of God's dealings with sinful man; that they were witnesses of the incarnation of the God-man; that they shall be God's reapers at the great harvest; and that now they are His "ministering spirits, sent forth to minister to them who shall be heirs of salvation." How different is this from all that the Koran teaches, with its mixture of Magian fancy and Talmudic lore. But the reason to us seems obvious, the solution easy—the Koran is human, the Bible divine.

frequently and sternly denounced in the Qurán than any other,"—The Rev. James Kennedy, "Christianity and the Religions of India," p. 231 (A.D. 1874).

We now come to the doctrine of the Koran concerning *Prayer.* In chapter seventy-three Mahomet inculcates this duty, and the desirability of apportioning to it certain stated times. Thus:—"O thou wrapped up, arise to prayer, and continue therein during the night, except a small part; that is to say, during one-half thereof; or do thou lessen the same a little, or add thereto, and repeat the Koran." "Verily the rising at night is more efficacious for steadfast continuance in devotion," "for in the daytime thou hast long employment."[1] And, again, "Regularly perform thy prayer at the declension of the sun, at the first darkness of the night, and the prayer of daybreak; for the prayer of daybreak is borne witness unto by the angels."[2]

Mahomet thought prayer so necessary that he used to call it "the pillar of religion," and "the key of Paradise." He continually insists on its practice in the Koran. The pious Moslem performs this duty five times every day. 1. Before sunrise; 2, at noon; 3, before sunset; 4, after sunset, during the short twilight; 5, when night has set in. Wherever he may be, in the desert, at home, in his shop, or in the crowded street, he steps aside, spreads out some little carpet or cloth, takes off his shoes, and, with his face turned towards the Kibla at Mecca, performs, sitting, standing, or prostrate, his solemn and picturesque devotions. Some repair to the mosques for this purpose, but this, owing to occupation or distance, is not always practicable, and does not seem to be considered important.

It is not to be understood that these five appointed

[1] Sura lxxiii. 1–7. [2] Sura xvii. 8.

times of devotion are strictly and universally attended to. Many of "the faithful" use no prayers at all; some pray only at sunrise and sunset, or attend the mosque on Friday at the public prayers.

Certain ablutions, called "the key of prayer," are directed to be used, not before *all* their prayers, but always when the worshipper is conscious of impurity. The ordinary purification consists in washing the hands and arms to the elbows, the head and face, and the feet to the ankles;[1] and all these acts must be conducted with certain short prescribed prayers for God's pardon and help, for deliverance at the last day and admission to Paradise. The greater purification is the lustration of the whole body on the occurrence of certain natural defilements.[2] When water cannot be procured, or its use, owing to sickness, would be dangerous, fine sand may be substituted.[3]

The "adzân," or call to prayer, is chanted from the minarets of the mosques by the Mueddzin, in words which allude to the majesty and unity of God, the mission and glory of Mahomet, and (at night) the superiority of prayer to sleep. The prayers which are used at the five seasons are said to consist of so many "rakaats" or genuflexions, occurring between short prayers, from four to eight in number, which are either taken from the Koran or otherwise appointed.[4]

[1] Sura v. 8, 9. [2] Sura iv. 46. [3] Sura v. 9.

[4] Suras i. cxii., the declaration of the unity, cviii., or some of the other shorter ones, are used; also selections from the larger. Conf. "Notes on Muhammadanism," xviii. Prayer 6, 63. Prayers from the Koran are entitled Farz; Sannat those founded on the teaching of Mahomet; and Nafal voluntary prayers.

On Friday, the day of public assembly, the same prayers are used, led by some Imam (antistes), who holds office at the mosque, for there is no order of men set apart for the purpose; and he usually reads, in addition, some set address (Khutbah), or preaches to those assembled.

Rosaries, consisting of ninety-nine beads (the number of the names of Allah), are frequently seen in the hands of the most zealous Moslems, and are used to count the ejaculatory prayers: such as "Praise be to God," "God is most great," &c., which are directed to be repeated a certain number of times. On the conclusion of the set prayers, the devout, sitting cross-legged at their ease, and with downcast eyes, may offer up any special prayer for which they have occasion.[1]

Women are taught that it is better for them to pray at home; they are absolutely excluded from some mosques, and are seldom seen in the others at the ordinary times of prayer. They join, however, in the festival of the Moharram, particularly on the

[1] In Mahometan countries, though there are no regularly-ordained clergy, still there are learned men specially appointed to expound the orthodox law in ecclesiastical, civil, and criminal cases. The chief of these are the Qazi (Cadi), the chief judge who passes sentence. (2) The Mufti, the official referee who supplies to the judge decrees (fetwa) in difficult cases, based on the Koran or the rulings of the great orthodox doctors. (3) Imam, appointed to read public prayers. (4) Moulvies, Moullas, Mujtahids, learned doctors and teachers of religion. The word sheikh, corresponding to presbyter or elder, is a title of respect. The Sheikh-ul-Islam in Turkey has much power, holds the ecclesiastical revenues, and is referred to by the Sultan as the highest authority in matters civil and ecclesiastical.

tenth day; and they accompany their husbands on the pilgrimage to Mecca.

A learned writer has remarked, "The utmost solemnity and decorum are observed in the public worship of the Moslems." "Never are they guilty of an irregular word or action during their prayers,"—"they appear wholly absorbed in the adoration of their Creator, without affected humility or a forced expression of countenance."[1]

In the thirtieth chapter, which belongs to this period, usury is forbidden, and this includes taking any interest for money. Thus, "Whatever ye shall give in usury, to be an increase of men's substance, shall not be increased by the blessing of God."[2] And, again, "Truly, selling is but as usury, and yet God hath permitted selling and forbidden usury." "Whoever returneth to usury they shall be the companions of hell-fire, they shall continue there for ever."[3] Lawful commerce is allowed; "God sendeth the wind"—"that ships may sail,"—"that ye may seek to enrich yourselves of His abundance by commerce, and that ye may give thanks."[4]

The thirty-first chapter of the Koran is entitled "Lokman," surnamed "the Wise"; an individual, around the circumstances of whose era, nationality, and parentage, such a crowd of fables and anachronisms have gathered, as to make it more than doubtful whether he ever really existed. He is introduced to us in the Koran, and an amiable and pious discourse is put into his mouth, addressed to his son, whom he advises to flee from polytheism,

[1] Lane, "Mod. Egypt.," i. 120.
[2] Sura xxx. 38.
[3] Sura ii. 276.
[4] Sura xxx. 45.

and to believe in one only God, to follow that which the Almighty reveals, not that which the fathers followed; to be constant at prayer, patient under affliction; to dread the day of judgment; and to avoid the way of arrogant and insolent men. This is a specimen of the artful way in which the prophet seeks to support his special doctrines, by making them part of the teaching of an ancient sage, and so investing them with his authority and credit.[1]

The other revelations of this period are chiefly made up of the stories of the Old Testament, adapted so as to support Mahomet's claims; and he does seem to have found means of gaining a fairly comprehensive idea of the leading facts of the Jewish histories. Curious fabulous additions, which will be noticed hereafter, taken from rabbinical legends, tradition, and other sources, are interwoven with them; but there can be little doubt, from whatever source he got his information, that many a secret hour must have been spent in study and composition to enable him to produce the revelations demanded by the pressing necessities of the hour, and the craving faith of his disciples.

As a specimen of the introduction of these Old Testament characters into the Koran, and of the jumble made of their history, which would often be unintelligible but for our knowledge of the sacred narrative, the following may be cited:[2]—"Jonas was also one of those who were sent by us; when he

[1] *Vide* D'Herbelot, art. "Locman-al-Hakim"; Sale, p. 335, note. Lokman and the Persian hero Rustum may probably be placed in the same category.

[2] Sura xxxvii. 133–142.

fled into the loaded ship, and those who were on board cast lots among themselves, and he was condemned, and the fish swallowed him, for he was worthy of reprehension. And if he had not been one of them who praised God, verily he had remained in the belly thereof until the day of resurrection. And We cast him on the naked shore; and he was sick! And We caused a plant of a gourd to grow up over him, and We sent him to an hundred thousand persons, or they were a greater number, and they believed: wherefore We granted them to enjoy this life for a season."[1]

Finally, as an example of the way in which Mahomet takes the fancies of the Talmudists, and the legends of the Haggidah, and reproduces them in the Koran, the following may be given. In the 148th Psalm, "the sweet singer of Israel," in the exuberance of poetic fervour, calls upon the heavens and all the angel host, the mountains and all hills, and even the "flying fowl," to join in praising the Lord. Occurring in a poem, such mode of expressing the gratitude of the Psalmist for God's goodness to him and to all creatures is natural and appropriate. The Talmudists, however, as was their wont, notwithstanding the palpable absurdity, have taken this passage in its bare literal sense, and Mahomet, accepting their interpretation, founds upon it this passage:—"We heretofore bestowed on David

[1] This reads much more like notes jotted down for a fuller history of Jonah, which have been accidentally incorporated with the Koran—a supposition not unwarranted by the way in which these compositions were kept by the prophet, and put together by his followers.

excellence from Us; and We said, O mountains, sing alternate praises with him; and We obliged the birds also to join therein."[1] And in a later sura it is repeated, "And we compelled the mountains to praise us with David, and the birds also: and We did this."[2]

In the Gospels only a few brief glimpses are afforded us of the manner of life of our blessed Lord during those quiet years at Nazareth, when, in obedience to his parents, from "sweet and holy childhood" to years of manhood He "increased in wisdom and stature, and in favour with God and man." But this mysterious veil of silence, which divine wisdom has drawn, was not respected by the fabulists of Christendom, who have surrounded His boyhood with innumerable stories of the exhibition of a marvellous and divine power. In the Arabic "Gospel of the Infancy," for instance, it is related how among His playmates He gave life to little sparrows which He had moulded out of clay, and when He clapped His hands they rose and flew away. Mahomet, by some means or other, possessed himself of this story, and in a late Medina sura reproduces it as part of the "preserved book."[3] Such, then, is as detailed an account as our space will allow of those parts of the Koran revealed up to the time of the imprisonment in the Sheb Abu Talib (A.D. 617).

[1] Sura xxxiv. 102. [2] Sura xxi. 79.
[3] Sura iii. 43.

CHAPTER VI.

LAST YEARS OF MAHOMET AT MECCA.—[A.D. 617–622.]

WE now take up the thread of Mahomet's history. Allusion has been made to the sufferings which he and his followers endured with patience, to their scanty supply of food consequent on their social isolation, and how this state of things went on for some three years. We read that, in order to bind firmly together the ranks of the adverse faction certain terms of union had been agreed upon, and to give the league a religious sanction, that this table of conditions had been hung up in the Kaaba. At the expiration of three years it was discovered, to the consternation of the confederates, that the documents had been destroyed by insects. This circumstance, to which a portentous meaning favourable to the new sect was at once given, aided by other reasons, probably of a family nature, detached from the league five of its chief supporters. This fact broke up the confederacy, released the imprisoned religionists, and restored them to their homes in comparative peace and safety.

It was at this time that Mahomet suffered the loss, by death, of two of his nearest and best friends—his wife, Khadija (A.D. 619), and his faithful uncle, the aged Abu Talib (A.D. 620).

Though Khadija was much older than the prophet, and though the custom of Mecca and his own revelations permitted polygamy, he is said to have remained true to her, and never to have wounded her heart or aroused her jealousy by taking a second wife during her lifetime. Deeply did he lament her loss, and to the day of his death honoured the memory of her goodness and of her early unwavering faith, and placed her name in the list of the four perfect women.[1]

The loss of Abu Talib he mourned much, though he is said to have died in unbelief, for it was to him a loss of great political moment. The whole tenor of his acts, and his sacrifices for his nephew, "stamp his character as singularly unselfish and noble."[2]

For a time Mahomet's uncle, Abu Lahâb, hitherto and afterwards his bitter opponent, undertook to take the place of Abu Talib, and to be his protector; but he was soon seduced by the hostile Coreish, and thus Mahomet and his followers became exposed to the unchecked insults and persecutions incited by Abu Sofian, Abu Jahl, and others; and being but a handful in the hostile city, were unable to cope with its rich and powerful chiefs.

At this critical period, either because he found it unsafe to remain in Mecca, or because he trusted that his message would find more acceptance else-

[1] Conf. Koran, sura lxvii. 11, 12. The names of these four women who reached perfection were Asia, wife of Pharaoh; Mary, daughter of Imran, the mother of our blessed Lord; Khadija, the wife of Mahomet; and Fatima his daughter, wife of Ali.—*Vide* Sale, note *ad loc.*

[2] Muir, ii. 195.

where, Mahomet, accompanied by his faithful freedman Zeid, set off to Tayif, a strongly fortified town inhabited by the Beni Thackif, situated some seventy miles to the east of Mecca.

There is something very touching in the view of the solitary wanderers as they set forth in faith and devotion. On they toiled, across sandy wastes, over burning rocks and barren hills, till they reached the heights of the Jebel Kora, where gardens, palm-trees, vineyards, and "fruits of plenty spread on every hand," made a welcome and refreshing contrast to the dreary wilderness through which they had passed, and cheered the visionary seer and his faithful comrade.

And so they descended into the valley of Tayif, which town at that time and long after was one of the great strongholds of idolatry. There a stone image, called "Al Lât," usually adorned with costly vestments and precious stones, was an object of worship and profound veneration, and was esteemed to be one of the daughters of God. Here for ten days Mahomet preached to unwilling ears, and met with nothing but opposition and scorn from the chief men, which soon spread to the populace. At last, with Zeid he was driven out of the town, and, maltreated and wounded, had to make for the foot of the hills, where he hoped to find shelter among the vineyards and to escape the pursuit of the infuriated rabble.

Driven thus forth from the city and worn out, they sat down under a vine in a garden belonging to two youths of the hostile Coreish, who had noticed the fugitives' forlorn plight, and touched by their sufferings sent them a dish of grapes. Refreshed by the welcome present, Mahomet set forward on his journey, and halfway to Mecca rested in the valley of Nakhla, where, as we have seen, the Genii heard him at night reading the Koran, and were converted. After a few days' rest at this place he returned to Mecca, wearied indeed and disappointed, but still strong in the belief of his divine mission.

Mahomet now found himself free from personal molestation, under the protection of Mutim, a chief of the blood of Abd Shams. His unsuccessful mission to Tayif, which became known to the hostile faction, procured for him a season of contemptuous toleration, more bitter, perhaps, to his lofty soul than active opposition.

At this time (A.D. 620) he entered into a double matrimonial alliance, taking to wife Sawda, the widow of one of his converts of the Coreish ; and being betrothed to Ayesha—the daughter of his bosom friend Abu Bekr—then only seven years of age.

But though thus pleasing himself in his domestic life, his outward circumstances were dark enough. His private means were straitened ; the consoling sympathy of Khadija and of Abu Talib was his no more ; for ten long years his life had been a scene of such care, anxiety, obloquy, and comparative failure, as must, at his age (for he was now fifty), have weighed heavily on his mind.

His fortunes, however, had reached their lowest ebb, when the tide suddenly turned, and in its flow bore him on beyond his most sanguine expectations. During the season of the annual pilgrimage, in the spring, Mahomet sallied forth, as was his wont, and preached to the assembled crowds.

When the usual ceremonies were drawing to a close, and the devotees had returned to the valley of Mina, he approached a "little group of six or seven," who proved to be strangers from Medina,[1] of the tribe of the Khazraj. To them he explained his doctrines, and urged them to accept a purer faith than that in which they were born. It would appear, indeed, that upon the dwellers in Medina idolatry had not so firm a hold as upon the Meccans, owing, perhaps, to their familiarity with the purer worship of the Jews, and also to the absence of any strong personal or political interest in the maintenance of the ancient superstition.

It is also believed by some writers that the Jewish hopes of a Messiah had penetrated to their Arab neighbours, and had awakened in them, torn as they were by intestine feuds, a yearning for a deliverer, so that they were ready to accept the one who came to them of Arab blood, of the sacerdotal caste, and who seemed likely to fulfil their highest hopes.

However this may be, it is certain that Mahomet's eloquent teaching found more congenial soil among them, and so they joyfully acknowledged his mission, and made profession of "the faith." To his new disciples he poured out the story of the difficulties and dangers of his position at Mecca, and inquired whether they would protect him at Medina. They

[1] The city of Yathrib, better known by its later name of Medina, lies some 250 miles to the north of Mecca. In and around it were large colonies and tribes of Jews, and from its proximity to Syria, the inhabitants doubtless must have formed some conception of a more spiritual religion than that practised at the Kaaba.

explained that their city was rent by opposing factions, that they could not therefore make him the promise he desired, but that at the next annual pilgrimage they would come and give him their answer.

And so they returned home, and spread his doctrine, and that with such success that "there remained hardly a family in Medina in which mention was not made of the Prophet."[1] It would even appear that the Jews favoured him, inasmuch as he had acknowledged the validity of their Scriptures, and taught some doctrines which they loved. Thus, from a variety of causes, Islam secretly and openly took deep root and spread in Medina.

Faithful to their promise, twelve of the new converts returned at the annual pilgrimage and formally acknowledged him as their prophet, and plighted him their faith, "agreeing to acknowledge but one God, to act morally and justly, not to kill their children, and to obey the Prophet in all things lawful." Such was the first pledge of Acaba, agreed to in April, A.D. 621. And so they returned to their native home, and the faith continued to spread in Medina, chiefly through the preaching of Musab-ibn-Omeir, a young and ardent Moslem, who had been sent thither by Mahomet at the request of the inhabitants. Their idols were thrown aside, many even of the hostile factions of the Aws and the Khazraj joined in the common devotions, and thus wonderfully was a purer theistic faith substituted for the old superstitions of the Arab population.

External events, too, favoured the fortunes of Islam. For many years the victorious arms of the

[1] Muir, ii. 210.

Persian Chosroes had humbled the Christian princes of the East; but in A.D. 621 an important and decisive victory gained by the emperor Heraclius, rolled back the tide of invasion from the shores of the Bosphorus, and the Cross triumphed over the fire-worship of the Magian invaders. This was, at the same time, a triumph for the theistic faith of Mahomet, and seemed in its mystical meaning to prefigure the downfall of Arabia's idolatrous rites, for in it true believers saw the sure accomplishment of a prophecy which their leader had uttered,[1] thus "The Greeks have been overcome by the Persians, but after their defeat they shall overcome the others in turn within a few years" — "Write, to God belongeth the disposal of this matter"—"And on that day shall the believers rejoice in the success granted by God."[2]

The fortunes and hopes of the dejected prophet having thus risen, his heart naturally went out to those who had acknowledged his mission. Mecca had rejected it, called him "liar," and his teaching "falsehood."[3] No converts were being added to the faithful few there; surely it must be the will of Heaven that he should leave them! The Meccans must have been given over to worship their idols, and to a reprobate mind; and what if his preaching were opposed to the evident signs of the Almighty? what if he were found to be fighting against the decrees of Allah? Such may have been some of

[1] Sura xxx., entitled "The Greeks—Al Roum"—properly the Romans.

[2] Conf. Kasimirski, "Koran," p. 343; Sale, notes, *ad loc.*; Muir, ii. 224; Freeman, "The Saracens," p. 24.

[3] Sura vi. 34-37.

the thoughts which occupied the mind of Mahomet as he reflected upon the hopeless prospect at home, and gazed longingly over the northern hills towards the city, where he was regarded as a revered apostle, and perhaps almost as a prince. And so, as he recalled the asylum which in past years the converts had found beyond the sea, the picture of a peaceful haven at Medina, and of crowds of enthusiastic and devoted followers, would grow still brighter and more alluring.

And therefore we cannot wonder that the little flock are bidden to prepare themselves for abandoning their homes, and that soon the will of Heaven is found to sanction, nay command, the step which they meditate of quitting the doomed city; thus, "they accuse thee, O Mohammed, of imposture, and follow their own lusts"—"and now hath a message come unto them, wherein is a warning from obstinate infidelity:"—"but warners profit them not; wherefore do thou withdraw from them."[1]

Thus the year A.D. 621 draws to its close, unmarked by any important event. The cry of the prophet is unheard in the streets, for his thoughts are far away. Revelations from Heaven come as occasion requires, by them the faithful are strengthened, but still more by the calm trust and undaunted attitude of their spiritual guide.

In the spring of the next year, during the holy months, there assembled at the national shrine at Mecca the usual crowds of busy devotees; but amidst the throng one group alone of about seventy persons need claim our regard. They are the new

[1] Sura liv. 2-6.

disciples from Medina, come to tell the prophet of their welfare, that the truth had found a ready reception, and that they were prepared to offer him a resting-place in their midst, and to conduct him from the idolatrous city.

Towards the close of the ceremonies, the ambassadors assembled secretly at the hill of Acaba, "a secluded glen" northward of Mecca, where, in order to escape the notice of the hostile Coreish, it had been arranged they were to meet the prophet, and formally pledge him their word. Before midnight Mahomet repaired to the place, accompanied by his uncle Al-Abbas, who (though he had not openly declared for the new faith) loved his nephew, and was anxious that his decision at this crisis should be wise and prudent. He therefore urged on the men of Medina not to raise hopes which they could not fulfil, nor to promise a protection which they might prove unable to afford. They replied that they were able, and fully determined, to secure his safety with their lives and fortunes; nay, more, to take him as their prophet and their master. Such was the "second pledge of Acaba,"[1] which took place in the March of A.D. 622. The protection thus offered and accepted, gained for the believers of Medina the title of "Ansâr," or Auxiliaries.

Some vague accounts of the midnight meeting, and of the important pact entered into between Mahomet and the men of Medina, as well as rumours of an early emigration of the Moslems from Mecca, reached the ears of the Coreish, and roused them to a renewal of such severities and persecutions, in-

[1] Muir, ii. 239.

cluding in some cases imprisonment, as hastened the departure of the believers to the city where they were assured of a friendly reception. By permission of the prophet the emigration began, and within two months—with the exception of Mahomet and Abu-Bekr and their households, and those who were forcibly detained in slavery—all had met with the cordial welcome and hospitality of their brethren at Medina.[1]

The devotion of the Moslems at the call of their faith and their prophet, and the sight of the abandoned dwellings, alarmed the hostile chiefs of Mecca; but their deliberations as to how they might effectually extinguish the growing sect, or counteract the bold step which had been taken, came to no definite result. The flight of his adherents had placed Mahomet more than ever in their power, yet they seem to have been unable to settle how to act under the unexpected emergency. Their deliberations, however, were made known to the prophet, and hearing that certain of their number were appointed to visit his house, he directed Ali to occupy his bed, threw over the youth "his red Hadhramaut mantle," and at once proceeded to the house of Abu-Bekr, who had already made the necessary preparations for their flight.

Passing the southern suburb of Mecca in the dusk of evening, they escaped to a cave on Mount Thaur, a lofty hill some six miles to the south-east. There they remained concealed for three days, till the search was somewhat relaxed. Food was conveyed to them at night by Abdallah and Asma, the

[1] Muir, ii. 247.

children of Abu-Bekr, and they had a plentiful supply of milk brought them by a faithful shepherd. There is, perhaps, no incident in the life of the prophet which more nearly touches the sublime, which sets his courage, his calm unwavering trust in God in a more exalted light than the story of this cave on Mount Thaur. If discovered thus alone on the barren mountain how easily might the assassin have executed his murderous work unseen by mortal eye. Pursuit was hot, and the less masculine soul of Abu-Bekr, fearful for the safety of the apostle of God, conjured up visions of approaching foes in each dark shadow of the fitful twilight and in every rustling leaf of the thorny acacias. "They be many that fight against us, and we are but two." "Not so, Abu-Bekr," replied the prophet; "we are but two, but God is in the midst a third."

The flight, pursuit, and the safety of the wanderers are, as might be expected, adorned with details of the miraculous protection of Heaven. Among these is the well-known story that for their safety a spider spun its web over the mouth of the cave; and on a tree which miraculously sprang up the brooding wood-pigeons, undisturbed, showed the pursuers that no one could have taken refuge within.[1] In one of the later Medina suras the before-mentioned circumstances are thus referred to:—"If ye assist not the Prophet, verily God will assist him, as He assisted him formerly, when the unbelievers drove him out of Mecca, the second of two: when they were both in the cave: when he said to his companion, God is with us" (Sura ix. 40).

[1] Conf. Sale, P. D., p. 51; Irving, p. 72; Muir, ii. 257.

Two camels had been provided by Abu-Bekr for their northern journey, and on the fourth day, leaving their place of retreat, they struck off westward towards the Red Sea, passed Bir-Osfan and Codred, and on the eighth day reached the rocky ridge whence the traveller looks down on the rich valley in which Medina lies. Their eyes, wearied with journeying under a meridian sun through barren and thirsty defiles, must have been refreshed at the sight which opened before them. They would look down on green fields, orchards, and palm groves, a scene to them of quiet, though of infinite beauty and repose. To the right the summit of Jebel Ayr; northward, beyond the valley, the granite mountain of Ohod, where afterwards the sword of Islam failed in the hand that wielded it; away to the south and east, till lost in the horizon, the plateau of Najd; and below the peaceful suburb of Coba, nestling amidst its palm groves.

Thither the travellers wended their way, and welcomed by the greeting of the exiles who had preceded them, and by the smiles and gratulations of the new converts, soon after alighted in Medina. Such was the celebrated "Hejira," or Flight of Mahomet from Mecca to Medina, from which the Mahometan world computes its era. He fled from the cave of Thaur on the 20th, and arrived at Medina on the 28th June, A.D. 622. Within a few weeks the members of the families of Mahomet and Abu-Bekr, who had remained behind at Mecca, set out leisurely and without molestation, to join the rest of the fugitives at Medina.

CHAPTER VII.

THE LATEST TEACHING AT MECCA.—[A.D. 617–622.]

I PROPOSE now to take into consideration those chapters[1] of the Koran which are thought to have been dictated during the last years of the prophet's residence at Mecca. In them we shall be able to trace the influence of external circumstances on his hopes and aspirations, and notice how they served to develop the scope of his teaching and the future of Islam.

In nearly the whole of these chapters we meet with wearisome repetitions of the same line of argument which he had taken up in the earlier suras. We encounter the same references to the unsuccessful mission of earlier prophets to the idolatrous nations of old, to show that the rejection of his words by the Meccans was to be looked upon as a mere repetition of the same want of faith, and, more than this, as constructively a proof of the validity of his mission. Hud sent to the Adites, Salah to the children of Thamud, Lot to the city of Sodom, Shoaib to the "Midianites of the wood," Abraham's unheeded preaching, and

[1] Muir, "Life of Mahomet," Appendix, vol. ii., gives the following sequence of the chapters :—46, 72, 35, 36, 19, 18, 27, 42, 40, 38, 25, 20, 43, 12, 11, 10, 14, 6, 64, 28, 23, 22, 21, 17, 16, 13, 29, 7.

Pharaoh's rejection of the words of Moses, were but so many types of his mission to the inhabitants of Mecca, and of their reception of him; and it is shown that calamities, similar to those which befell the nations of old, will assuredly overwhelm them if they continue to prefer their idols to the worship of God, and still reject his warnings. His religion, he tells them, is freely offered, for he asks no reward; and he assures them that he is not a preacher of any new doctrine, no innovator, but sent at God's command to instruct them in that faith which is the only true one, and the rejection of which will bring upon them the judgment of Heaven. Thus: "He hath ordained you the religion which He commanded Noah, and revealed to thee, O Mohammed—and Abraham and Moses and Jesus, saying, Observe this religion" (Sura xlii. 11).

During this period it cannot be doubted that Mahomet found opportunity, generally we may believe during the quiet hours of the night, for prosecuting his study of the Jewish histories; for he reproduces the minute details of the stories of Moses (Sura xxviii.), of Joseph (Sura xii.), and of others, though all are more or less mixed up with legends and apocryphal additions of his own. In his treatment of the Scriptures he shows no comprehensive grasp of Old Testament teaching; his knowledge is purely superficial, touching only the outside shell of facts, and these are often distorted and strained to suit his own purposes, and abound in fanciful and incongruous details and fables.

Thus he tells the story of the "Seven Sleepers"

dormant in the cave for 309 years, to illustrate God's care of those who avoid idolatry (Sura xviii.); the golden calf in the wilderness is made to low (Sura xx. 90); the children of Israel are seduced to idolatry by a Samaritan (*Idem*, 7, 8); Joseph is stated to have been sorely tempted by the "Egyptian's wife," and the women of Egypt cut themselves for their love of his beauty (Sura xii. 24); Joseph satisfies his father that he is still alive in Egypt by sending him an inner garment, the smell of which Jacob recognizes, and is by it cured of his blindness (Sura xii. 95); the odour of the vest is borne on the air to the aged patriarch from Egypt to Canaan (Sura xii. 94); the people of the "City near the sea" are changed into apes for fishing on the Sabbath (Sura iii. 166); Abraham, for speaking against the idolatry practised round him, is cast into a burning pile—but God makes the fire cold (Sura xxi. 69); the winds are said to have been subject to Solomon, and to have run at his command (*Idem*, 81); the latter asserts himself to have been taught the language of birds (Sura xxvii. 16), and talks with a lapwing which expresses its belief in the unity of God (*Idem*, 20–26); a terrible genius (in org Efreet) brings to Solomon, in the twinkling of an eye, the queen of Sheba's throne (*Idem*, 40); Job strikes with his feet, and a fountain springs up as a liniment for his sores; he is also ordered to beat his wife with rods (*Idem*, 41–43); &c.

Such are a few specimens of the frivolous incidents mixed up with the graver story of the doings of the old patriarchs. A perusal of the Koran can alone give the reader any just idea of the tedious manner in which certain "special subjects" are repeated over and over again, with but trivial variation. In the midst of all these revelations there occur here and there excellent moral sentiments to which no exception can be taken. Thus the duty of helping the poor, of relieving the needy traveller, and of doing justice to the orphan, is insisted on. The love and honour due to parents from their children, the performance of covenants, and the use of just weights, form part of the believer's duty. Liberality is commended, profuseness condemned. The Prophet points out, how, at the end of the world, our words, our thoughts, nay, the very use of our eyesight, will be brought into account, and he states how desirable it is for the true believer to love God, to pray to Him, and to walk humbly in His sight (Sura xvii.).

On the occurrence of such sentiments in the Koran, it may be well to remember, that no civilized heathen nation ever existed, in which just, beautiful, and sublime sentiments were not known and recorded in their sacred books. The works of Confucius abound in them; the ancient writings, still held in veneration by millions in Hindostan, furnish many passages of a morality as discriminating and high-toned as any to be found in the book of Mahomet. But it is the juxtaposition of other pernicious opinions, claiming equal inspiration and authority, which have ever tended to neutralize what was just and true, and to render them without any efficient practical influence.[1]

[1] Conf. M. Williams's "Indian Wisdom," pp. 3, 38, 58, 512, *et seq.*

We may notice at this time an important change in the attitude to be assumed by believers. They are now permitted to repel the ill-usage of their enemies and draw the sword as a defensive weapon; thus, "Permission is granted to those who take arms against the unbelievers, for that they have been unjustly persecuted and turned out of their habitations injuriously, and for no reason than because they say our Lord God" (Sura xxii. 40). In a few short months we shall find how the aggressive sword of Islam is permitted to succeed this defensive warfare.

He is, as usual, profuse in his praise of "the perspicuous," "the glorious Koran," sent down from Heaven; and he now ventures to appeal to his knowledge of the Old Testament histories as a proof of its authenticity. He represents himself as ignorant and illiterate, but that God directly instructed him. Thus: "We (God) relate unto thee a most excellent history, by revealing unto thee this Koran, whereas thou wast before one of the negligent" (Sura xii. 2). And again: "Say, it is a weighty message from which ye turn aside. I (Mahomet) had no knowledge of the exalted princes when they disputed about the creation of man; it hath been revealed unto me only as a proof that I am a public preacher" (Sura xxxviii. 67–70).

He explains his imperfect knowledge, and how it is that he is still ignorant of some parts of the old Scriptures, thus: "We (God) have sent a great number of apostles before thee: the histories of some of whom we have related unto thee, and the histories of others we have not related unto thee." In face of the above assertions, if his words are to bear a literal meaning, we know not how to acquit Mahomet of something of conscious misrepresentation; for it is incredible that he could, by any tortuous reasoning, construe the results of his own study to mean direct inspiration, or that the knowledge which he gained from human agents was the teaching of God.

In the sixth sura we meet with certain positive precepts regarding food, where "that which dieth of itself, or blood poured forth, or swine's flesh, or that slain in the name of some other god" are forbidden as an abomination (Sura vii. 118). The ancient rites and ceremonies of the temple at Mecca, the pilgrimage, the circuits round the Kaaba, the accustomed sacrifices and vows, are still to continue in force, except only that the faithful "depart from the abomination of idols in associating any other with God" (Sura xxii. 27–32). The horrible practice of infanticide, viz. burying their daughters alive, which prevailed among certain of the Arab tribes, is condemned and forbidden, and those who slay their children threatened with perdition (Sura vi. 138, and lxxxi. 8, 9).

To this period, "when visions of a journey north ward flitted before his imagination,"[1] belongs the story of the celebrated "Night Journey" [Lailat-al-Miraj] of the prophet from Mecca to Jerusalem, on the winged steed Al-Borâc, and thence by a ladder of light above the seven heavens to the very presence of God, whom "he saw by the Lote Tree, beyond which there is no passing" (Sura liii. 13, 14). For

[1] Muir, "Life of Mahomet," ii. 219.

the details of this revelation,[1] with all its later embellishment of curious and extravagant fiction, drawn from the legends of the Haggidah, and the dreams of the Midrash and the Talmud, the prophet cannot, in fairness, be made responsible. His simple account of what was probably only a dream prompted by his waking thoughts, is as follows:—"Praise be unto Him, who transported his servant from the sacred temple (at Mecca), to the farther temple (at Jerusalem), the circuit of which we have blessed, that we might show him some of our signs" (Sura xvii. 1). I have already alluded to the repeated direction of Heaven to the prophet "to withdraw from the unbelievers," which occurs in many of the suras,[2] revealed when thoughts of a sanctuary at Medina were present to his mind, and when he was on the eve of his departure from Mecca.

Lastly, we have proof that he was now begin ning to extend his study from the books of the Old to those of the New Testament; if, indeed, it may be assumed that he ever consulted the original texts, and did not content himself with gaining his knowledge from apocryphal sources, which have distorted his views and tinged his words with their own colouring. It may, I think, be assumed that Mahomet got his information chiefly through these and Jewish channels, and hence we shall see no cause to wonder that he has adopted the teaching of those who "killed the Prince of Peace," and "desired

[1] For a curious account of the "night journey," *vide* Prideaux, "Life of Mahomet," pp. 41–51; also Muir's "Life of Mahomet," ii. 219–222; D'Herbelôt, art. "Borak"; Lane, "Modern Egyptians," ii. 225.

[2] Conf. Suras xliii. 89, vi. 112.

a murderer to be given unto them";[1] and find no reason to marvel at his incorrect views of the Saviour, and of the introduction into the Koran of puerilities and apocryphal stories found in the "Gospel of the Infancy."[2]

If such were, indeed, the case,[3] it would account to some extent for his unwavering hostility to the doctrine of the divine Sonship, the mystery of the Holy Incarnation of Him whom the Jews crucified, and which would form a constant theme of denial for their unhallowed tongues. The Scriptural doctrine of the Three Persons of the Godhead contained in the Old Testament, and unfolded in the New, is, as might have been anticipated, strongly condemned and repudiated by Mahomet. Thus, "Believe in God and His Apostles, and say not there be three Gods; forbear this, it will be better for you. God is but one God" (Sura iv. 169); and again, "They are certainly infidels, who say, God is the third of Three; for there is no God besides one God" (Sura v. 7).[4]

It will be well in this place to consider what the teaching of the Koran is regarding the birth, the attributes, the mission, and death of our blessed Lord; and for this purpose I consider it best to use the words of the book itself. The nineteenth sura,

[1] Acts iii. 14, 15.

[2] *Vide* Sale's "Koran," pp. 42, 118, notes.

[3] We cannot doubt that many reasons of the strongest kind would induce Mahomet to keep the sources of his information, and the names of his instructors (if such he had), as secret as possible. That he was suspected of having teachers we know.

[4] It seems clear that Mahomet had no correct grasp of the Christian doctrine of the tri-unity of the Godhead.

entitled "Mary" (Maryam), opens with an account of "the mercy of the Lord to Zacharias," and tells of his age and infirmities, his "fearing his nephews," his childless state, his prayers for an heir, who in the person of John is granted him, and how that son was endowed with "wisdom and purity of life." Then is given the "story of Mary, when she retired from her family to a place towards the East—and We, God, sent Gabriel unto her—a messenger of the Lord—to give her a holy Son" (Sura xix. 16—19). Another account is, that "The Angels said, O Mary, verily God sendeth thee good tidings, thou shalt bear the *Word*, proceeding from Himself; His name shall be Christ Jesus, the Son of Mary; but she answered, Lord, how shall I have a son, since I know no man" (Sura iii. 40–42). The account thus continues, "She preserved her virginity, and unto her we breathed of our Spirit, ordaining her and her son for a sign unto all creatures" (Suras xxi. 91, and lxvii. 12).

"Wherefore she conceived Him; and she retired aside with Him in her womb to a distant place; and the pains of childbirth came upon her near the trunk of a palm-tree. She said, Would to God I had died before this, and had become a thing forgotten and lost in oblivion" (Sura xix. 22, 23). But she is comforted by God eats the ripe dates which fall from the tree, and drinks of a rivulet miraculously provided; and then brings the child to her people, carrying Him on her arm (Sura xix. 28). They accuse her of incontinence, and she makes signs to the infant to answer them, "whereupon the child said, Verily I am the servant of

God;[1] He hath given me the book of the Gospel, and hath appointed me a prophet. And He hath made me blessed—and dutiful towards my mother—this is Jesus, the Son of Mary; the Word of Truth, concerning whom they doubt. It is not meet for God that He should have any Son; God forbid" (Sura xix. 31–36).

Little information is given regarding the boyhood and manner of life of Christ. "God," it is stated, "strengthened Him with His Holy Spirit,[2] and taught Him Scripture and wisdom and the law and the Gospel, and appointed Him His apostle to the children of Israel" (Sura iii. 43). The performance of certain miracles is attributed to Him, speaking to men in His cradle, making clay birds to fly, giving sight to the blind, life to the dead, and cleansing the lepers; all done, not by His own power, but "by the permission of God" (Sura iii. 41, and v. 110).

The child Jesus, in His cradle, is made to utter words which are meant to support the Mahometan cultus, thus "Wheresoever I shall be: God hath commanded me to observe prayer and to give alms so long as I shall live" (Sura xix. 32). The feeding of the multitudes in the wilderness and the institution of the Last Supper are, it would seem, confounded in the Koran: thus, "The apostles said, O Jesus, son of

[1] The first words put into the mouth of the child Jesus are intended to make Him deny His divine Sonship; and the prominent way in which His human nature is indicated in the words "Son of Mary" is doubtless intended to serve the same purpose.

[2] Suras ii. 81, v. 109.

Mary, is thy Lord able to cause a table to descend from heaven? we desire to eat thereof, that we may know that thou hast told us the truth. And Jesus said, O God, our Lord, cause a table to descend unto us from heaven, that the day of its descent may become a festival unto us" (Sura v. 112–114).

With regard to the Death of our blessed Lord, the Koran denies that He was really put to death: thus, "And they" (the Jews) "say, Verily, we have slain Christ Jesus, the son of Mary, the Apostle of God! Yet they slew Him not, neither crucified Him, but He was represented by one in His likeness; they did not really kill Him, but God took Him up unto Himself, and God is mighty and wise" (Sura iv. 156). There is a further account of the crucifixion: thus, "And the Jews devised a stratagem against Him (Jesus); but God devised a stratagem against them"; and this passage continues thus: "God said, O Jesus, Verily I will cause thee to die, and I will take thee up unto Me" (Sura iii. 47, 48). These apparently contradictory passages have given much trouble to the Mahometan commentators, who explain that "God's stratagem" was in stamping the likeness of Jesus on another person, who was apprehended, and suffered the ignominious death in His stead. The death which He is to suffer will, they say, occur "when He shall return into the world before the Last Day."[1]

[1] At Medina, in the "Hujrah," or chamber where Mahomet is buried, a vacant tomb is left for "Seyedna Isa-bin-Maryam" (Jesus Christ) at his second coming, where, on the fulfilment of His mission, He is to be buried. Cf. Burton, "El Med. and El Mec.," ii. 89; Lane, "Modern Egyptians," i. 93.

The Saviour, they add, was allowed, after God took Him up, to descend for the purpose of comforting His mother and disciples, and telling them how the Jews had been deceived! Other explanations are given of His death: that it was a spiritual death to all worldly desires; or a real one lasting a few hours.[1] On this head it should be added that certain heretical Christian sects,[2] at the very beginning of Christianity, denied that Christ Himself suffered, but that Simon the Cyrenean, or Judas, was crucified in His place.

Finally, the Koran, while acknowledging Christ Jesus to be "honourable in this world and in the world to come, and one of those who approach near to the presence of God" (Sura ii. 40), asserts that "He is no other than a servant whom God favoured with the gift of prophecy" (Sura xliii. 59), and "is not to be associated in that worship which is due to God only" (Sura ix. 31). Such, then, is the teaching of the Koran regarding the birth, the life, and the death of our Lord and Saviour.

It is painful to read such words, but, such as they are, they will give the Christian reader a just conception of Mahomet's claim to inspiration, and will satisfy him that the prophet of Mecca knew nothing of the true nature of that Christianity about which he ventures to write. Though he speaks of our Lord always in terms of the highest respect, and makes mention of certain of His miracles, he had no heart to know the higher and more wondrous miracle of His

[1] Conf. Sale's "Koran," p. 43; Kasimirski, "Koran," p. 60, note.

[2] The Basilidians, the Cerinthians, and the Carpocratians.

pure life, and of His love which sought by the death on the Cross "to bring many sons to glory." With the strangest inconsistency he calls Him, "The Word of Truth," yet refuses to listen to the gracious words which fell from His lips; acknowledges that He was "strengthened by the Spirit of God," yet repudiates the honours which He claims; and thus we find His divine nature attacked, His precious death denied, and no allusion made to that Redemption which was purchased by His sufferings on Calvary.

Vain, however, and illusory are his, and all other human efforts to explain away the clear teaching of Scripture, to rob the Son of Man of His divine honours, and to leave Him but an inferior and delegated authority. The eternal purpose of God revealed to man in the Word of Truth will still stand firm and unshaken before such attacks, and vindicate its authority when they shall have all perished under the weight of their own inconsistencies and errors.[1]

[1] It need hardly be remarked that repudiation of the divinity of Christ, and the denial of His death, strike directly at the root of our Christian faith. Christ's divinity once set aside, and His mission lowered to that of an Apostle only, room would be left for similar successors, and a plausible justification of Mahomet's pretensions would be thus provided (conf. Bishop Horsley's Sermons, vol. iii. pp. 12, 13). The greatest inconsistency is manifest in the Koran, which, while acknowledging the authority of the Old and New Testaments, and professing only to be a continuation of God's revealed will, yet virtually gives these very Scriptures the lie, by repudiating all the leading dogmas of the Christian faith.

CHAPTER VIII.

MAHOMET'S CAREER AT MEDINA.—[A.D. 622–632.]

WE now return to take up the story of the prophet's fortunes at Medina. He remained four days at Coba; and having satisfied himself that the general enthusiasm, and the curiosity to see the man whose name was so great in Arabia had lulled the active passions of contending faction, he made his almost triumphal entry into Medina. Seated on his camel, he allowed the animal unchecked to select the spot for his future residence. The place thus chosen was a piece of waste ground within the eastern limits of the city, and near the house of one Abu Ayub,[1] under whose roof he resided for seven months. His table was amply supplied by the voluntary offerings of the Faithful. The work of erecting a mosque and suitable dwellings was the first business of the prophet and his followers. The ground, which he bought, was cleared and levelled, and a temple, some hundred cubits square, arose on the site where now stands the large and beautiful mosque which bears his name.[2]

[1] This Abu Ayub was afterwards (A.D. 672) killed at the siege of Constantinople, and gave his name to the "Mosque of Ayoub," at the northern end of the Golden Horn.

[2] For a detailed description of the Masjid-al-Nabi at Medina, *vide* Burton, "El Meccah and El Medinah," vol. ii. chap. xvi.

Round the temple rose, in process of time, apartments for his wives as they were gradually added. At first two only were built, one for Sawda, and a second for Ayesha, then in her tenth year, who for the consummation of her nuptials took possession, with unostentatious pomp, of that chamber which was destined to be the burial-place of her husband. Regular services were commenced, Mahomet or some vicar appointed by him leading the daily public prayers; whilst on Friday, at the mid-day office, all the Faithful were expected to be present.

In his marriage with Ayesha, which took place in the winter of A.D. 622–623, Mahomet gave practical effect to his previous sanction of polygamy, on which the following remarks may be made. It is not apparent, from any facts we know, that Mahomet is personally to be blamed for the step he thus took. In the histories of the Old Testament, of which he had been no idle student, he would find numerous examples of its practice by patriarchs and kings, with the tacit approval, certainly without the expressed reprehension, of a higher power; and though condemned by the purer teaching of Christianity, we cannot assume that he was aware of this fact. Moreover, he found it sanctioned by the example of the Jews, universally the custom in Arabia, and practised by his most devoted followers; and it may be concluded, either that its practical working failed to impress him with the desirability of interfering with its existence, or, if in any way alive to its evils, that he shrank from the task of setting himself in opposition to this, the most cherished privilege of his pleasure-loving disciples.

Therefore, though it is to be doubted whether he ever seriously contemplated the practical results of his legislation on this subject, having in the Koran sanctioned the practice of polygamy, he must be held responsible for the long train of degrading consequences which have followed the licence thus established, "which has undoubtedly proved, in its ultimate results, one of the greatest and most fearful evils of the Mahometan system."[1]

It may be well in this place to consider what the teaching of the Koran is on the subject. In the 4th sura, entitled "Women," among various directions regarding their years of orphanage, inheritances, chastity, and the forbidden degrees, permission is given to the Faithful "to take two, or three, or four, and not more" women as wives (verse 3), and in addition to these as concubines, the slave-girls, "which their right hands possess" (Sura lxx. 30),[2] that is, purchased or made captive in war. In reality, the number of wives is practically unlimited, as the Koran allows an almost unchecked power of divorce and exchange (Sura iv. 18). The action of the husband, who is expressly stated to be superior to the wife, is

[1] Freeman, "History of the Saracens," p. 53.

[2] Muir, "Life of Mahomet," ii. 140, note; iii. 305. So long as this unlimited permission of cohabitation with their female slave continues, it cannot be expected that there will be any hearty attempt to put a stop to slavery, whatever form it takes, in Mahometan countries. Though Mahomet, in some respects undoubtedly ameliorated the condition of slaves, there is sufficient proof that he looked upon it as a permanent institution (cf. Sura xxiv. 33; Muir, iv. 239, 321; and Hughes, Notes on Mahommedanism, p. 185).

nearly uncontrolled.[1] He may repudiate his wives without any assigned reason, and without warning; may, if apprehensive of disobedience, rebuke, imprison, and strike them (Sura iv. 28); and against this the dishonoured spouse has almost no means of redress.[2]

Exposed to the tyranny of her husband, and treated as a kind of plaything,—a being formed for lust and labour, to be capriciously flung aside on the least provocation, or in a moment of anger, or for mere dislike,—she is worse than a slave. Such a system is intolerable, indeed, to a feeling heart, and consistent only with that social degradation of the sex which is its inseparable attendant. The very caprice of the husband is encouraged by the permission granted of twice repudiating and twice receiving back the same woman. If he a third time divorce her, she cannot again become his wife till she have married, cohabited with, and been divorced by some other man (Sura ii. 230).

The majority of Mahometans, constrained by poverty or custom, content themselves with one wife; and though such marriages may be, and doubtless are, often happy ones, still the wife, under the licence of the Koran, has continually hanging over her head the apprehension of divorce, and this cannot but prove an abiding source of uneasiness to her. However exemplary and devoted her conduct, she may at any moment be called upon to quit her home and her children, and see her place occupied by some younger

[1] Lane, "Modern Egyptians," vol. i. 139 *et seq.*

[2] She can claim the balance of her dowry, generally a very insignificant sum, and maintenance for three months.

and more favoured stranger. Some Mahometans make a habit of continually changing their wives. We read of young men who have had twenty and thirty wives—a new one every three months; and thus it comes about that women are liable to be indefinitely transferred from one man to another, obliged to accept a husband and a home wherever they can find one, or in case of destitution, to which divorce may have reduced them, resort to other more degrading means of living.

Further evils follow this pernicious system, which cannot here be particularly recorded. Enough has been said to show the practical working of the rules of the Koran on the important subject of marriage and divorce—rules which strike at the root of all morality, brutalize man, degrade women, and render the Christian ideal of domestic life an impossibility; and yet for them is claimed a divine origin, and they are emphatically called "the ordinances of God declared to people of understanding"[1] (Sura ii. 230).

On this subject it may be well to remark that the popular idea of the exclusion of women from the Paradise of Mahomet is quite erroneous. Though no details of the delights in store for them are vouchsafed by the prophet—for on this point he observes a prudent reticence—we are informed that "God will lead the believers of both sexes to the gardens of delight."[2]

[1] Conf. Deut. xxiv. 3, 4, for the purer and stricter regulations of the Mosaic law of divorce. Conf. Sale, D. P., sec. vi.; Muir, iii. 300–307.

[2] Conf. Sura xlviii. 5; iv. 123. The reader will call to mind Gibbon's remarks on Mahomet's silence in this particular.

It cannot be imagined that Mahomet's arrival in Medina, and his powerful position there, as the actual prophet and prince over his own sect, and as possessing a dominating authority in the city, proved in all respects acceptable to those who either disbelieved his claims, or viewed with jealousy the rising power of the stranger. And so it was that, both among the Jews, who were numerous at Medina, and the Arabs, who still dallied with the old idolatry, elements of antagonism came to light. The "Disaffected,"[1] as they are called, are bitterly inveighed against in the Koran; hell-fire, it is stated, is to be their portion; and a whole sura (lxii.) is devoted to an exposition of their lying and their wicked conduct in seeking "to set the inhabitants" against the prophet of God.

With the Jews, on his first arrival, he made a treaty of alliance, by which the free exercise of their worship, and the possession of their rights and property was guaranteed; but it soon became apparent that the two sects could not exist harmoniously side by side. Mahomet's conduct in his dealings with the rival religionists is very instructive. In his earlier inspirations he had spoken of them as the chosen of heaven, and their books as having divine authority, and had, as we have seen, heaped together facts drawn from their sacred canon to illustrate the truth of his mission. He had acknowledged that a strict compliance with the Mosaic ritual was compatible with future salvation; he had fixed upon *their* holy place

[1] Sura iv. 144. The original ("Munaficun") is by Sale rendered by the word "Hypocrites."

at Jerusalem as the Kibla of his faith; and in many ways sought to conciliate them and gain their weighty testimony to the truth of his claims: but all had been in vain; he found that they disbelieved his assertions, mocked at his revelations, and gave out that in their prophetic books no authority for his pretensions was to be found.

Mahomet was not without resource. He employed his old weapons against them; accused them of rejecting their Messiah; asserted that they systematically concealed all the passages foretelling his appearance; and that on them as on their fathers, who had rejected the preaching of Noah and of Abraham, was fallen a thick darkness,—eyes that would not see, ears that would not hear the latest message of Heaven delivered by his lips. To embittered feelings succeeded menacing words; and the Jews of Medina soon felt the power and hostility of the prophet's arm.[1]

Established thus in a position of security, Mahomet began to cast his eyes abroad upon other scenes. His strength was to go forward, and to find employment for the eager passions of his disciples, who, in the chilly atmosphere of Medina, sighed for a return to their warmer home at Mecca. In the winter of A.D. 622–23, and during the ensuing year, various plundering expeditions, under Hamza, Obeida, and the prophet himself, left Medina, chiefly with the object of intercepting the caravan trade between Mecca and Syria; and though few prisoners and

[1] It was about this time that the "Kibla," as above related, was changed from Jerusalem to Mecca.

little booty were taken, the Coreish had reason to know that they could no longer reckon on immunity from molestation in their future mercantile expeditions.

In November 623 an expedition of eight of the "Fugitives" was sent to lie in wait in the valley of Nakhla; and within one of the four sacred months surprised a Meccan convoy. One man was killed, two of the Coreish taken prisoners, and the camels with their loads carried off to Medina. "This was the first booty the Mussulmans obtained, the first captives they seized, the first life they took";[1] and though the attack had been made in the holy month Rajab, which even the Pagan Arabs respected, a convenient revelation justified the supposed desecration, and established that to kill the unbelievers is less grievous than idolatry, and to war in the sacred months than to obstruct the way to the holy temple.[2]

Thus as regards the idolaters the scabbard was thrown away from the aggressive sword of Islam, all former words of forbearance cast to the winds. To this period may probably be attributed the Divine command, "to fight against the idolaters until the religion be the Lord's alone";[3] the fearful are reproved, war encouraged, nay commanded, though it be irksome; and Paradise guaranteed as the reward of those who fall in the fight.[4] We shall find, at a later period, how this command was extended to regulate the treatment of Christians and Jews.

[1] Muir, iii. 75.
[2] Conf. Sura ii. 214.
[3] Sura ii. 189.
[4] Sura xlvii. 4-7.

The affair at Nakhla was followed by the celebrated battle of Badr. In January 624, on the return journey of the Meccan caravan from Syria, Mahomet determined to attempt its capture, and for this purpose set out from Medina with 305 of the "Fugitives" and "Ansâr," and encamped by the fountains. Though Abu-Sofian succeeded by forced marches in placing his convoy beyond danger, it was settled that a body of troops, numbering about 950, which, under Abu-Jahl, had been sent from Mecca to his assistance, should advance and measure swords with the Moslems. The battle began with a series of single combats, in which Hamza—the Lion of God—Ali and Obeida encountered and slew Otba, Walid, and Shuiba. The engagement then became general, "the army of the Faithful was borne forward by an enthusiasm which the Coreish were unable to withstand";[1] their line, notwithstanding their superior number, began to waver, and the retreat quickly became an ignominious flight. Forty-nine of the Meccans perished, and an equal number were taken prisoners: on the side of Mahomet fourteen fell.

Of the prisoners some were slain on the field, and others afterwards put to death in cold blood; for we learn that on the evening of the battle, in the valley of Otheil, Mahomet sanctioned the slaughter of Nadr; and two days after that of one Ocba, for the comforting sight of whose blood he returned thanks to Heaven. A justification of these unwarrantable deeds was subsequently vouchsafed, and is

[1] Muir, iii. 105.

found in the Koran.[1] A dispute regarding the distribution of the booty necessitated an especial revelation, which established the principle that one-fifth part was to be "for God and his Apostle," and the remainder distributed equally between "those who had fought and those who had stayed under the ensigns."[2]

Such was the memorable battle of Badr, insignificant, perhaps, in the numbers engaged, but stupendous in its ultimate results. The prophet had drawn the sword, and submitted the proof and justification of his claims to its capricious decision, for on its victory or defeat the cause of Islam was to stand or fall.[3]

On his return to Medina, Mahomet found his position much strengthened, and he assumed a dictatorial tone which demanded unhesitating obedience. We can hardly doubt, too, that the sight of the spoils and the prisoners, whose money ransom was permitted, provided his disciples with proofs of the divinity of Islam as convincing as the laboured arguments and measured cadences of the Koran. With the Jews it was different. They were unimpressed with the validity of such mundane reasoning, refused to relinquish the faith of their fathers, and still ridiculed the prophet; and so the angry feelings of the two

[1] Sura viii. 68–76.

[2] Sale's note, "Koran," sura viii. p. 139. Also conf. 1 Sam. xxx. 20–25. The prophet's fifth part was the "Sadacat," "for himself and his family, the orphans, the poor, and the traveller" (Sura viii. 5).

[3] The victory is attributed to the direct assistance of God, and it is intimated that 3,000 angels fought for the Moslems (Sura iii. 13, 119).

sects grew more and more intense; secret assassinations, stimulated by Mahomet, struck them with an undefined terror, showed the dangerous brink on which they stood, and convinced them that a plausible excuse only was wanted for open rupture.

This soon presented itself. An Arab girl, the wife of a convert, was insulted by a youth of the Beni-Cainucâa, one of the chief Jewish tribes in Medina; bloodshed followed, and taking advantage of this circumstance, the whole tribe was attacked, proscribed, and banished. Their lands, houses, and goods were confiscated, and divided among the victors. In the course of the same year (A.D. 624) one Kab-ibn-Ashraff, a Jew who had annoyed the Moslems with his verses, was at Mahomet's instigation assassinated under circumstances of the blackest treachery.[1] In his domestic relations Mahomet had to mourn the death of his daughter Rockeya. During the winter months he married his fourth wife, Haphsa, the daughter of Omar; and in January, A.D. 625, was born his grandson Hasan, the son of Fatima and Ali.

At Mecca the tidings of the disastrous defeat at Badr aroused the bitterest feelings of anger, and passionate cries for vengeance arose on every side, and in particular from Hind, the wife of Abu Sofian, whose father, brother, and uncle had fallen. On the opening of the year 625 alarming rumours of an attack on Medina reached the ears of the Prophet, and soon the news was sent him by his uncle Abbas that a force of 3,000 men had taken the northern

[1] Conf. Muir, iii. 143.

route. In ten days the Meccan army reached Dzul-Halifa, four miles south of Medina, and thence striking to the north, encamped to the west of Ohod, an isolated mountain, some three miles north-east of the city, and there began to ravage the fields. On the side of the Moslems, it was at first decided to await the attack within the city; but bolder counsels prevailed, and Mahomet, clad in armour, led out his army of 1,000 men, and halted for the night. At early dawn he advanced on Ohod, and occupied the sloping ground at the western side, where his rear was protected by its rising spurs. Here he was abandoned by Abdallah, chief of the "Hypocrites," with 300 of his followers.

Of the Meccan army, the right was commanded by Khalid, in after days so valiant a champion of the faith he now sought to destroy, the centre by Abu Sofian, and the left by Ikrema, the son of Abu Jahl, whose death at Badr he thirsted to avenge. The standard was borne by Talha, who had inherited the privilege from his ancestor Abd-al-Dar. The battle, as seems to have been usual at the time, began with a succession of single combats, in which Hamza and Ali slew their opponents, and the engagement then became general. The Meccans were carried away before the fierce onslaught of the Moslems; but the latter pressing too hotly, the fortune of the day was entirely changed by Khalid. The prophet, who had vainly attempted to check the fugitives, was twice wounded and fell, but succeeded in reaching a place of safety among the ravines of Ohod. Seventy-four of the Moslems lay dead on the field; and among others the gallant Hamza, who had been brought lifeless to the ground by a wild negro, whom the fury Hind had, by the promise of freedom, thus engaged to satisfy her revenge. After the fight she gloated over the body of her victim, tore out the heart, and gnawed it with her teeth! On the evening of the battle the Coreish retreated, and Mahomet, after burying the dead, amidst the wailing of distress, began the homeward march. I have before made mention of the revelation which came to still the murmurs of those who had lost relatives at Ohod.

During the year 625 various expeditions were sent abroad to propagate the faith and to check hostile movements among neighbouring tribes; and in these murder and treachery play an important part. From certain political complications Mahomet continued, without any adequate reason, to pick a quarrel with the Jewish tribe of the Beni Nadhir, whose stronghold, Zohara, lay a few miles to the south of Medina. Refusing to listen to any explanation, he bid them, in the name of the Lord, gó forth from their homes on pain of death. They were obliged to obey his stern mandate and give up their houses and lands, which were forthwith divided among the "Fugitives." The Koran contains a song of praise to God, in which the Prophet records his thankfulness for having been enabled successfully to accomplish the spoliation and banishment of this unoffending people.[1]

I return to the domestic affairs of the prophet.

[1] Conf. Sura lix. 1–8 *et seq.*; Muir, iii. 208; W. Irving, chap. xxi.; and Sale's notes, *ad loc.*

In December, 625, he married his fifth wife, Zeinab, daughter of Khozeima, whose husband had fallen at Badr. In January, 626, a sixth, Om-Salma, widow of one of the heroes of Ohod; and six months later (June), Zeinab-bint-Jahsh, the divorced wife of his adopted son Zeid. On a certain day, Mahomet entering unexpectedly the house of Zeid, had a momentary glimpse of the charms of his beautiful wife, and uttered a cry of passionate admiration. The circumstance was reported, and the disciple, by an immediate divorce, enabled the prophet to add a new bride to his harem.

By these marriages—for he had then six living wives—the legal number allowed to the Faithful[1] had been overstepped, and, moreover, his alliance with the wife of his adopted son was considered highly improper, if not incestuous. But Mahomet had an easy and effectual method of silencing present scandal and avoiding further complication by an additional Sura to the Koran; thus: "O Prophet, we have allowed thee wives—and also the slaves which thy right hand possesseth—and any other believing woman, if she give herself, and the Prophet desireth to take her to wife. This is a peculiar privilege granted thee above the rest of the believers" (Sura xxxiii. 49–51). It is impossible to avoid wondering at the strange credulity of his followers, who, with seemingly undiminished faith, allowed him the aid of inspiration as a pander to his personal predilections.

Regarding the fair Zeinab, it was laid down

[1] Sura iv. 3.

that she was joined to the prophet by the will of Heaven, to show that believers commit no sin in 'marrying the wives of their adopted sons."[1] The special revelation given forth to sanction this marriage is, by the ablest writer on the subject,[2] justly stigmatized as an act of "impious effrontery"; and another author is obliged to confess that his relaxation of the marriage rules in his own favour "is the greatest stain, and an indelible one, on his memory."[3]

In the same chapter[4] certain rules are laid down regarding the conduct to be observed by visitors. Guests and strangers are not to enter his habitations uninvited; they are to use no familiarity, but are quickly to depart; they are to speak to his wives "from behind a curtain"; are to give the apostle of God no uneasiness in these particulars; and, above all, are forbidden "to marry his wives after him at any time,—verily that would be an enormity in the sight of God."

An expedition (December, 626) to the wells of Muraisi, north of Jiddah, on the seashore, resulted in the defeat of the Beni-Mustalick and the capture of a

[1] Sura xxxiii. 37. Zeinab boasted to the other wives of the prophet that *her* marriage alone had been ratified in Heaven. Zeid is the only "companion" mentioned by name in the Koran (Kasimirski, p. 347). [2] Muir, iii. 230.

[3] Bosworth Smith, "Mohammed," p. 88. Mr. Smith thinks Mahomet "may have justified himself to his own mind by the Ethiopian marriage not condemned in the case of Moses." He appears to assume that this was a second wife of Moses; but there is no proof of this, or that Zipporah is not identical with the "Cushite woman" (Forster, "Geog. of Arabia," vol. i. p. 12). [4] Sura xxxiii. 53.

large number of persons. Among the captives was Juweiria, the beautiful daughter of the chief, who, on a question of her ransom, appealed to the prophet, was viewed with eyes of desire, and, after embracing the faith, became his eighth wife.

The expedition is memorable for the adventure which, for a time, compromised the reputation of Ayesha. By accident she was left behind on the return journey to Medina. On the arrival of the convoy, she was found absent from her litter, but soon after appeared seated on the camel of one Safwan. Scandal was soon busy in putting the worst con struction on her conduct. The prophet was distressed at the misadventure which had befallen his best beloved wife, and for a month forsook her society; after which a revelation established her innocence and restored her to his arms. This circumstance gave rise to the Moslem law regarding adultery, which necessitates the production of four witnesses to substantiate the charge against "women of reputation," and further directs that they who make a false accusation of this kind are to be beaten with fourscore stripes.[1] If convicted, the Koran lays down that wives "are to be imprisoned in a separate apartment till death release them."[2] By the Sunnah, the punishment, according to a supposed abrogated passage, was directed to be death by stoning.[3] In Egypt, the usual punishment of the offence is drowning. The

[1] Sura xxiv. 4. Mahomet consulted Ali about Ayesha. At first he seemed inclined to suspect her chastity. She never forgave him.

[2] Sura iv. 19.

[3] Conf. Sale, P. D., sec. 3. Comp. St. John viii. 4-11.

legislation of the Koran in this particular, and as regards murder, theft, mutilation, &c., owing to its cruelty, inconsistency, and inadequacy, has, in many particulars, been neglected, if not altogether set aside, in the more advanced countries where Islam prevails.[1] Fornication is forbidden, is declared to be wickedness and an evil way,[2] and is to be punished, in either sex, by 100 stripes. Marriage with a harlot is forbidden to true believers.[3] But however salutary Mahomet may have considered these regulations, the almost unlimited licence in marriage and divorce enables offenders to set them at defiance.[4]

The opening of the year 627 (March) saw the prophet threatened with a formidable danger. Abu Sofian, the chief of Mecca, had engaged a number of Bedouin tribes to assist him in making a united attack on the rising power, and had advanced on Medina with some ten thousand men. The Moslems intrenched and fortified their city, and were content to repel the attack from behind their walls. During a fruitless siege of fifteen days, mutual jealousy and disaffection paralyzed the efforts of the besiegers. A terrific storm which fell on their camp hastened their retreat, and filled them with the apprehension that the very elements were leagued on the side of the apostle of God.

Then follows a crime memorable for its atro-

[1] *Vide* Monier Williams, "Indian Wisdom," p. 273. Code of Manu.

[2] Sura xvii. 34.

[3] Sura xxiv. 3.

[4] *Vide* Lane, "Modern Egyptians," ii. 98, and note. See also i. 141, 409, *et seq.*

city and for the view it affords us of the sanguinary principles which, at this time, regulated Mahomet's conduct. On the arrival of the confederates they had found means to win over the Beni Coreitza, a Jewish tribe, whose possessions lay exposed to attack, and who had indeed entered into terms of alliance with Mahomet, but whose compact with him "was of a weak and precarious nature." Though their defection, which amounted to little more than neutrality, at such a critical moment, might have warranted Mahomet in expelling them from their possessions it by no means justified the slaughter which followed. On the retreat of Abu Sofian they were besieged, reduced to extremity, and had to surrender at discretion. Their fate was left to the decision of a chief of the Beni Aws, and by him the men were adjudged to death, and the women and children to slavery. In companies of five or six the horror-stricken Jews, to the number of some 800, were led out, and, in Mahomet's presence, butchered in cold blood! One shudders at the recital of this horrible transaction, and at the picture of the man, who, unmoved to pity, nay more, with fierce denunciation,[1] could witness the awful carnage to its end—a deed in its atrocity comparable to the Massacre at Melos,[2] and to the act of that sanguinary wretch who directed the blood-bath of Stockholm.

Yet in the Koran this accursed slaughter is applauded, attributed to divine interposition, and pronounced consonant with the love and compassion

[1] Muir, iii. 277. [2] Thucydides, v. 116.

of the All-merciful![1] Muir justly remarks that "the butchery of the Coreitza leaves a dark stain of infamy on the character of Mahomet."[2] Among the captives was a Jewess (Rihana), whose charms had caught his eye. Refusing the position of a wife, she became his slave and concubine, on his return from the spot where he had just witnessed the bleeding corpse of her husband, and the destruction of all her male relatives!

The truth is that Mahomet had by this time become deeply, nay irreconcilably hostile to the Jews of Medina. At first indeed he had availed himself of their aid in establishing himself in their midst, but now, when success enabled him to slight their assistance, he threw them contemptuously aside, and eagerly availed himself of any plausible excuse for their destruction. In addition, his dark suspicions were aroused that a lingering illness which troubled him was due to certain "Enchantments" they had directed against him. The 113th Sura is a short prayer to God for deliverance from "the mischief of the night when it cometh on, and from the mischief of women blowing on knots, &c."[3] We may gather

[1] Sura xxxiii. 22–27; and Sale's note; W. Irving, p. 116.

[2] Muir, iii. 284. Bosworth Smith (Mohammed, p. 90) calls this act, "in all its accessories, one of cold-blooded and inhuman atrocity."

[3] In accordance with their prophet's belief in magic, incantations, &c., the use of charms and amulets is universal among Mahometans, to counteract the influence of enchantments, disease, the evil eye, &c. Of these charms, the most potent is a copy of the Koran; but the Faithful, as a rule, content themselves with certain verses only, invoking God's protection against

from this prayer some knowledge of the superstitious fears, and that dread of the Unseen, which formed so curious a feature in the complex character of Mahomet.

I pass over the remaining events of the year (A.D. 627), which are a repetition of the usual expeditions for plunder, for dispersing robber bands, or for repelling the encroachments of other tribes for pasturage. During this time, we know, assassinations were deliberately planned by Mahomet, and the perpetrators blessed and rewarded; and we also meet with instances at this period of the barbarous mutilation of captives. On this head the Koran directs "that the enemies of God and of his Apostle shall be slain, or crucified, or have their hands and feet cut off, or be banished the land."[1] Theft is to be punished thus: "If a man or a woman steal, cut off their hands."[2] The law of "life for life, eye for eye," and that wounds are to be punished with the like,[3] is retained in full force. Thus, then, we have the Jewish law of retaliation—abolished by the Christian dispensation[4]—revived in the Koran, and

the devil. Of these, Suras xii. 64, xv. 7, xxxvii. 7 may be noted. The first of these is as follows:—"God is the best protector." The texts are written out and enclosed in amulets, and worn on the neck or arm. Bits of the "Kiswa," or silken covering of the Kaaba, which is renewed annually, are considered very efficacious.

[1] Sura v. 37. [2] Sura v. 42. [3] Sura v. 49.

[4] St. Matthew v. 38, 39. Conf. Lane, "Modern Egyptians," i. 146: "At El Medinah justice is administered in perfect conformity with the Shariat, or Holy Law." (Burton, ii. p. 281, note.) See also Sale, "Koran," sura v. p. 87, note.

express sanction given to the barbarous practice of mutilation.

The recurrence of the holy month, Dzul-Caada, of the next year (Feb. 628), recalled to the mind of Mahomet and of his followers thoughts of the customary pilgrimage, and of their homes at Mecca, from which they had been excluded for six years. To gratify the wishes of his disciples, and to remind them that the ceremonies of the Kaaba, apart from idolatry, were included in their faith, he determined to lead his followers to the holy shrine. Numbering some 1,500 men they left Medina, but, when within two days' march of Mecca, their advance was checked by the Coreish, and Mahomet, turning to the west from Osfan, encamped at Al Hodeibia, on the border of the "Sacred territory."[1] At this spot, a treaty, called "the truce of Hodeibia," was concluded, which stipulated that all hostilities should cease for ten years, and that for the future the Moslems should have the privilege, unmolested, of paying a yearly visit of three days to the holy shrine. After sacrificing the victims, Mahomet returned to Medina.

As about this period (A.D. 628) Mahomet sent embassies to certain foreign sovereigns, inviting them and their subjects to embrace Islam, it may be well to consider the political condition, at the time, of the countries bordering on Arabia.

The royal dynasty of Persia belonged to the race of the Sassanidæ, of whom the most illustrious, Chosroes, surnamed Nushirvan, reigned at the time of

[1] The "sacred territory" (Haram) extends to a distance of some seven to ten miles round Mecca.

Mahomet's birth. After the fall of the Emperor Alexander, Persia had been subject in succession to the Macedonian kings of Syria—the Seleucidæ—and to the Parthian monarchs; but, after six centuries of bondage, the foreign yoke was broken, and Persia became subject to kings of indigenous birth.

Their religion was the Magian creed of Zoroaster, which, though acknowledging only the two great opposing powers of light and darkness, of good and evil, of Ormuzd and Ahriman, had fallen from its original purity, and the sacred fire had become the visible symbol of idolatrous worship.

Chosroes—called also Khosru Parviz—the Persian King, to avenge the murder (A.D. 602) of his friend Maurice, Emperor of Constantinople, attacked the tyrant Phokas, who had seated himself on the throne, and continued the war against the Byzantine empire for more than twenty years. Heraclius, son of the Exarch of Africa, deposed and slew Phokas; and after a variety of fortunes totally overthrew the Persians in the decisive victory of Nineveh (A.D. 627). Chosroes was soon after murdered by his son and successor Siroes (Feb. 628).

To Siroes and Heraclius ambassadors were sent by Mahomet. The former on receipt of the prophet's letter tore it to pieces; the latter (who at the time was on a pilgrimage from Edessa to Jerusalem, as a thanksgiving for his victory) received the despatch with much more courtesy, but probably threw it aside, as "the production of some harmless fanatic".[1]

[1] Muir, iv. 53.

Egypt and Syria had for centuries been portions of the Roman Empire, but, though professing the Christian faith, they had adopted a form of it "alien from the standard of Roman and Byzantine orthodoxy."[1] In both provinces the Nestorian and Jacobite heresies had taken deep root, and other elements of discord there were, which rendered their loyalty to the central power weak, and ready to be broken at the approach of the first resolute invader.

On the arrival of the envoys, Muckonckas, the Roman governor of Egypt, treated them with honour, and sent as presents to the prophet a white mule and two Coptic girls. Of the latter, the fair features and curling hair of Mary captivated the heart of Mahomet, and she became his concubine. In Syria, the embassy was treated with contempt by the Christian Prince of Ghassan. In Yemen, which before this time had become a dependency of the Persian Court, better success awaited his ambassadors. The governor, Badsan, who then resided at Sanā, freed from his allegiance by the death of Chosroes, signified his adhesion to the prophet. The messengers to the Court of Axum in Abyssinia were well received, a favourable answer returned, and the remaining exiles brought back to Medina.[2]

In the autumn of the year (A.D. 628) he set on foot an expedition against Kheibar, a town 100 miles to the north of Medina, inhabited chiefly by

[1] Freeman, "The Saracens," p. 20.

[2] Among these was Om-Habiba, a widow, the daughter of his arch-enemy, Abu Sofian. She became Mahomet's tenth wife on his return from Kheibar.

Jews, whose wealth and rich domains promised an abundant harvest of plunder. One by one their fortified villages fell into his hands, and driven at last to extremities they were obliged to give up their citadel—Camuss. Kinana, their chief, was tortured to disclose his wealth, and then beheaded; and the dark suspicion rests upon the prophet, that the well-known beauty of Safia,[1] Kinana's recently married wife, was the secret cause of her husband's execution. Immediately after his death she was summoned to the prophet's presence, who "cast his mantle round her," and she became his ninth wife. While still at Kheibar Mahomet narrowly escaped being poisoned. A dish of kid had been prepared for him, and though he had eaten only a mouthful before he perceived that it had been tampered with, he felt the effects of the poison to his dying day.

The advent of the holy month, Dzul-Caada, of the next year (Feb. 629), was eagerly expected by Mahomet and his followers, for then, according to the terms of the truce of Hodeibia, they might, without molestation, visit the holy city, and spend three days in the performance of the accustomed rites. The number of the faithful swelled on the approach to nearly 2,000 men; and the Coreish thought it best to retire with their forces to the heights overlooking the valley. Seated on his camel

[2] Sura xliv. 11, is supposed to be directed against his other wives for their mockery of Safia, the Jewess. Mahomet was much attached to her, and bid her retort that "Aaron was her father, Moses her uncle, and Mahomet her husband" (Sale's "Koran," p. 418, note).

Al Caswa, which eight years before had borne him in his flight from the cave of Thaur a hunted fugitive, the prophet, now surrounded by joyous crowds of disciples, the companions of his exile, approached and saluted the holy shrine. Eagerly did he press forward to the Kaaba, touched with his staff the Black Stone, seven times made the circuit of the holy house, seven times journeyed between Safa and Marwa, sacrificed the victims, and fulfilled all the ceremonies of the lesser pilgrimage.[1]

While at Mecca he negotiated an alliance with Meimuna, his eleventh and last wife. His marriage gained him two most important converts—Khalid, the "Sword of God," who before this had turned the tide of battle at Ohod; and Amru, destined afterwards to carry to foreign lands the victorious standards of Islam.

The services of these two important converts were quickly utilized. An envoy of Mahomet to the Christian Prince of Bostra, in Syria, having been slain by the chief of Muta—a village to the south-east of the Dead Sea—a force of 3,000 men under his adopted son Zeid, was sent (Sept. A.D. 629) to exact retribution, and to call the offending tribe to the faith. On the northward march, though they learnt that an overwhelming force of Arabs and Romans—the latter of whom met the Moslems for the first time—was assembling to oppose them, they resolved resolutely to push forward. The result was

[1] Conf. Muir, iv. chap. xxii.; Irving, chap. xxvii. For Kaaba conf. Suras ii. 119–121, xxii. 27–30; for Safa and Marwa, Sura ii. 153.

their disastrous defeat and repulse. Zeid and Jafar, a brother of Ali, fell defending the white banner of the prophet. Khalid, by a series of manœuvres, succeeded in drawing off the army and conducting it without further loss to Medina. A month later, however, Amru marched unopposed through the lands of the hostile tribes, received their submission, and restored the prestige of Islam on the Syrian frontier. Mahomet deeply felt the loss of Zeid and Jafar, and exhibited the tenderest sympathy for their widows and orphans.

The defeat at Muta was followed, in the south, by events of the greatest moment to Mahomet Certain smouldering hostilities between tribes inhabiting the neighbourhood of Mecca broke forth about the end of the year. These were judged to be infractions of the treaty (some of these tribes being in league with the Coreish), and were eagerly seized upon by Mahomet as justifying those designs upon Mecca which the success of his arms and the dominion he possessed over numberless tribes in the north, in the Hejaz, and Najd, now made it easy for him to carry out.

Having therefore, determined to attack his native city, he announced his intention to his followers, and directed his allies among the Bedouin tribes to join him on the march to Mecca. Although he took every precaution to prevent his preparations becoming known, the news reached the ears of the Coreish, who sent Abu Sofian to deprecate his anger and to induce him to abandon his purpose. Humiliation and failure were the only result of this mission.

On the 1st January, A.D. 630, Mahomet's march

commenced, and after eight days through unfrequented roads and defiles, the army, swelled to the number of 10,000 men, halted and lighted their camp-fires on the heights of Marr-al-Tzahran, a day's march from the sacred city. The prophet had been joined on his march by his uncle Abbas, and on the night of his arrival Abu Sofian again presented himself and besought an interview. On the morrow it was granted. "Has the time not yet come, O Abu Sofian," cried Mahomet, "for thee to acknowledge that there is but one God, and that I am his Apostle?" He answered that his heart still felt some hesitancy; but seeing the threatening sword of Abbas, and knowing that Mecca was at the mercy of the prophet, he repeated the prescribed formula of belief, and was sent to prepare the city for his approach.

The Moslems made their entry from four different quarters, and, with the exception of the detachment under the command of Khalid, met with no opposition. Seated on Al Caswa, and in the pilgrim garb, the prophet entered the city repeating verses of the Koran. Having approached the Kaaba, he touched the Black Stone and made the seven prescribed circuits. The custody of the key (Hijaba) he continued in the family of Othman, a descendant of Abd-al-Dar, and the cup of the well in that of Abbas, in whose family it remains to this day. Without delay orders went forth to sweep away all the idolatrous relics from the Holy House, and Hobal and its fellows were thrown down and destroyed.

The conduct of Mahomet in the treatment of his native home was marked with much generosity and good sense, and places his character in a very favourable light. Some three or four persons only, and those guilty of crime, were put to death, and then a general amnesty was proclaimed. Ikrema, son of Abu Jahl, and the fury Hind both experienced his lenity. Parties were sent out to destroy the idols around; and in the valley of Nakhla, the grove of Al Ozza and its weird priestess were destroyed by Khalid.[1]

Another circumstance should be mentioned, as reflecting much credit on the conduct of Mahomet at this time. A number of the Beni Judzima, a tribe professing Islam, had fallen into the hands of Khalid, and having on a former occasion plundered and slain his uncle, he revenged himself by ordering the execution of some of the prisoners. Mahomet, on hearing of the circumstance, called Heaven to witness that he was innocent of the crime, and forthwith sent Ali to make recompense for the murders and to restore the booty. Aroused, it may be, at the news of this unprovoked and wanton slaughter, the great tribe of the Hawazin, in alliance with the Beni Thackif, whose stronghold was at Tayif, the Beni Sad, and other tribes, entered into a league to resist the power which threatened to overwhelm the whole peninsula. Assembling with their families and flocks and herds at Autas, a valley between Mecca and Tayif, they encountered the forces sent against them in the narrow defile of Honein (February, A.D. 630). By the suddenness of the attack they caused a panic among the Moslems, whose flight was with difficulty stopped

[1] W. Irving, p. 154.

by the voice and example of Abbas. The result of the conflict, however, was the defeat of the confederate tribes and the capture of their wives, children, and cattle. Mahomet then advanced to attack the strong fortress of Tayif. Once before, it will be remembered, he had visited this idolatrous city and been driven from its walls, and now again the strength of its fortifications and its ample resources enabled it to defy all his efforts. After two weeks the siege was raised; and having performed the ceremonies of the Lesser Pilgrimage, he returned to Medina (March, 630).

In the distribution of the booty which had been taken, much dissatisfaction was felt. But here, again, the tact and good feeling of the prophet enabled him to silence all disaffection, and to prevail on the army to release the prisoners, at the intercession of the Beni Sad, among whom his childhood had been spent. The victory of Honein and the boastful confidence of the Moslems is alluded to in the Koran, thus: "God hath assisted you in many engagements, and at the battle of Honein, when ye pleased yourselves with your multitude, but it was no manner of advantage unto you,—then did ye retreat and turn your backs. Afterwards God sent His security (Shechina) upon His apostle and upon the faithful, and sent down troops of angels which ye saw not" (Sura ix. 25, 26).

On his return from the conquest of Mecca, Mahomet, then in his sixtieth year, was gladdened by the birth of a son by his concubine Mary the Copt. This child of his old age was doubly precious, as, with the exception of his daughter Fatima and her children, all his other descendants were dead. But from the day of its birth domestic quarrels troubled the peace of his harem. His other wives, jealous of the good fortune of Mary, who was a slave, murmured at the preference shown her, and their whispered complaints soon found occasion for open expression. Entering unexpectedly one day into her private room, Haphsa there surprised Mahomet with Mary, and her indignant feelings found vent in such bitter reproaches and threats of disclosure as induced him to promise that for the future he would separate from the favourite. Discovering that Haphsa, contrary to her promise, had made the circumstance known to Ayesha, he separated from them, and soon was granted a divine message, in which Heaven was made to administer a rebuke to his wives, and threaten them with divorce, and to state that the Lord can easily provide the prophet with other wives who would prove better, more pious, and more submissive to his will.[1] This especial revelation effectually extricated Mahomet from his domestic embroilment, was piously submitted to by his wives, accepted by his followers, and is to this day regularly read by the faithful as the word of God!

The conquest of Mecca was followed by the gradual submission of Arabia and the acknowledgment of the spiritual and temporal supremacy of the prophet throughout the entire Peninsula. Indeed, in the complex system which he had established, the spiritual and secular functions were

[1] Sura lxvi. 1–15.

intimately blended and involved in each other, and whilst in his humble home at Medina he retained still the simple manners of his earlier years, which at his time of life he had probably no inclination to alter, he exercised all those regal and sacerdotal powers which the victorious arms of his lieutenants, or the voluntary submission of the most distant provinces of Arabia, had caused to be universally acknowledged. Tax collectors were appointed to receive the prescribed offerings or tithes, which generally amounted to "a tenth part of the increase."[1]

The city of Tayif, as we have above seen, trusting to its natural strength, constituted itself a centre of disaffection; but at last driven to extremities, and seeing that all the neighbouring tribes had one by one submitted, its Chief, after a vain attempt to obtain some relaxation in the rules of Islam, consented to the destruction of the adored idol Lât, and adopted the new faith.

It was during the time of the next yearly pilgrimage[2] (March, 631), that Mahomet issued an important command, the crowning stone of the system he had raised, which shows at once the power he wielded and the strong hold his doctrines had already taken throughout Arabia. Refusing to be present himself during the ceremonies of the pilgrimage, he commissioned Ali to announce to the assembled multitudes in the valley of Mina, that at the expiration of the four sacred months the prophet would

[1] Muir, iv. 171.

[2] For a detailed account of the ceremonies of the pilgrimage, *vide* Burton, vol. iii. chap. xxviii.

hold himself absolved from every obligation or league with idolaters; that after that year no unbeliever would be allowed to perform the pilgrimage, or to visit the holy places; and further, he gave direction that either within or without the sacred territory war was to be waged with them, that they were to be killed, besieged, and laid in wait for "wheresoever found." He ordains, however, that if they repent and pay the legal alms they are to be dismissed freely;[1] but as regards "those unto whom the Scriptures have been delivered" (Jews and Christians, &c.) "they are to be fought against until they pay tribute by right of subjection, and are reduced low."[2]

Such, then, is the declared mission of Islam, arrived at by slow though inevitable steps, and now imprinted unchangeably upon its banners. The Jews and Christians, and perhaps the Magians,—"people of the book"—are to be tolerated, but held in subjection, and under tribute;[3] but for the rest, the sword is not to be sheathed till they are exterminated or submit to the faith which is to become "superior to every other religion."[4]

About the middle of the year (A.D. 631) a heavy grief fell upon Mahomet in the death of his little son Ibrahim, then about 15 months old. He fondly trusted that this child might be destined to transmit his name to posterity; but now these hopes were frustrated, and with a broken heart he followed

[1] Koran, sura ix. 1-5.

[2] Sura ix. 29.

[3] For its amount, *vide* Muir, iv. p. 215, note.

[4] Koran, sura ix. 35.

the beloved remains to the cemetery of El Bakia.[1] No spot more sacred than this is visited by the devout pilgrim to Medina. There lie, with the exception of Khadija, all the prophet's wives, the "Mothers of the Faithful," as they one by one passed away. There in his untimely grave lies Othman, the third Caliph; and there is seen the sepulchre of Abbas, the ancestor of those mighty princes who, on the ruin of the house of Omeya, held high state in Baghdad. There are the tombs of Halima the prophet's nurse, of three of his daughters, and of the murdered Hasan, his grandson, and there are interred many of the pious dead who are accounted martyrs, princes, and imams in the calendar of Islam. In this ground, then, the little Ibrahim found his last resting-place.

Few incidents in the life of the prophet, illustrative of the growth of Islam remain, which need claim our attention. I have endeavoured in what has already been written to give the reader a clear and accurate account of the manner in which his religion was begun, developed, and consummated; and how in all its wonderful growth it took so deep a colouring from the love, the hatred, and the ambition of Mahomet himself. And it has seemed to me that in showing its intimate association with his own story, I should best present a life-like picture of the mighty spiritual empire which claims him as its founder.

[1] For a full account of "El Bakia," *vide* Burton's "El Meccah and El Medinah," ii. 301. Fatima is buried in the Hujrah of the mosque at Medina. Halima's intercession with Mahomet, for his good offices, is invoked at her tomb.

As the approaching shadows of death begin to fall across his path, it is pleasing to notice from many circumstances that the natural magnanimity of his character more distinctly asserts itself, and forms a bright and pleasing contrast with the unscrupulous deeds of his earlier career at Medina. Though abating nothing of his exalted pretension to be the very apostle of God, though claiming for Islam a universal supremacy which was to brook no opposition, and submit to no diminution, he yet exhibits a calm submission to the will of God, and a perfect reliance on His unmerited mercy for admission to the Paradise of the Faithful.[1]

On the return of the sacred month (March A.D. 632), Mahomet, accompanied by all his wives, selected his victims, assumed the pilgrim garb, and set out, on what is called "The Valedictory Pilgrimage" to the holy places, from which every trace of the old superstition had been removed, and which, in accordance with his orders of the previous year, no idolater was to visit. Approaching the Kaaba by the gate of the Beni Sheyba, he carefully performed all the ceremonies of the "Omra" or "Lesser Pilgrimage," and then proceeded to consummate those of the greater. On the 8th of the holy month Dzul-Hijja, he rode to the Wadi Mina, some three miles east of Mecca, and rested there for the night. Next day passing Mosdalifa, the midway station, he reached in the evening the valley in which stands the granite hill of Arafat. From the "summit he spoke to the pilgrims regarding its sacred precincts, an-

[1] B. Smith, "Mohammed," p. 103.

nounced to them the perfecting of their religion," offered up the prescribed prayers, and hurried back to Mosdalifa for the night. On the 10th proceeding to Mina, he cast the accustomed stones, slew the victims brought for sacrifice,[1] had his head shaved and his nails pared, ordering the hair, &c., to be burnt; and the ceremonies ended, laid aside the pilgrim garb. At Mina, during his three days' stay, he preached to the pilgrims, called them to witness that he had faithfully fulfilled his mission, and urged them not to depart from the exact observances of the religion which he had appointed.[2] Returning to Mecca, he again went through the ceremonies of the Omra, made the circuit of the temple, drank of the well Zem Zem, prayed in the Kaaba, and thus, having rigorously performed all the ceremonies, that his example might serve as a model for all succeeding time, he returned to Medina.[3]

The excitement and fatigue of his journey to the holy places told sensibly on his health, which for some time had shown indications of increasing infirmity. In the death of Ibrahim he had received a blow which weighed down his spirit; the poison of Kheibar still rankled in his veins, afflicted him at times with excruciating pain, and bowed him to the

[1] Called "The Ransom."

[2] At Mina, Mahomet directed that the months of pilgrimage should be fixed according to the lunar year.

[3] Conf. Muir, iv. 235 *et seq.* Also Burton, vol. iii., for details of the pilgrimages. See also "Chambers's Miscellany," vol. x. No. 148, which gives a condensed account of Burckhardt's visit to Mecca.

grave. His life had been a hard and a stirring one, and now the important affairs of his spiritual and temporal kingdom, and the cares of his large domestic circle, denied him that quiet and seclusion for which he longed.[1]

It was about the end of May (A.D. 632) that he was attacked with a violent fever, which, though abating at times, was the beginning of his last illness. During the course of the malady, one sleepless night, he paid a visit to the cemetery of El Bakia, there remained long in prayer for forgiveness, and for the dead, whose quiet rest he envied, and to whose peaceful state he asserted himself to be hastening. The fever continued for some seven or eight days, and left him but little strength once more to address his followers in the mosque. To them tradition makes him to have announced his approaching dissolution, and to have told the weeping crowd that from the free choice of life and death, offered him by Heaven, he had selected "to depart and to be near his Lord"; and then commending the refugees of Mecca to the Medina converts, he returned to the

[1] During the year the pretensions of two impostors (among others) claiming the possession of prophetic powers caused him trouble and anxiety. One of these, Maseilama, found his proposals "to divide the earth" indignantly rejected by Mahomet, and himself stigmatized as a liar. He and his followers were crushed in the Caliphate of Abu Bekr. The other, Aswad, an Arab of wealth and influence, revolted and overran Najram, took the town of Sanâ in Yemen, and subdued the whole peninsula from the Hejaz to the Persian Gulf. His career was suddenly brought to an end by assassination, about the time of Mahomet's death.

room of Ayesha. His illness increasing he deputed Abu Bekr to lead the public prayers, and this was generally understood to intimate, that in the event of his death, he designed him for his successor.

About the 8th of June he had regained sufficient strength to make a final visit to the mosque. Viewing with joy the devotion of his followers, who, on the news of his illness had assembled in crowds, he proclaimed that he had made lawful to them only what God approved, that each one of them must work out his own acceptance with God, inasmuch as he himself had no power to save them; and after discharging some small claims, he returned exhausted and fainting to Ayesha's room. With his head on her lap he prayed for assistance in his last agonies, and for admission to the companionship of God. Ayesha tried in every way to soothe the sufferings of his last moments. Ejaculatory words at intervals escaped his lips, "Eternity of Paradise!"—"Pardon!"—"The glorious associates on high!"—and then all was still. The prophet of Mecca was dead.[1]

[1] Minute details of the death-bed utterances of Mahomet will be found in the larger works of his life. Nearly all rest on tradition subsequently collected, and are more or less open to the suspicion of having been invented, or coloured by the rival sacerdotal and political factions which in a few years convulsed the Caliphate,—Omeyades, Alides, Abbassides, and the party of Ayesha; Shias and Sunnis seeking by the prophet's utterances to support their political pretensions. Conf. Muir, iv. pp. 279, 280; W. Irving, pp. 182, 183; Lamartine, "H. de T.," vol. i. p. 268.

CHAPTER IX.

MAHOMET'S TEACHING AT MEDINA.—[A.D. 622–632.]

I HAVE still briefly to consider the general teaching of the Medina Suras.[1] Many of the chapters of this period are spun out to great length, and contain repetitions of former revelations which call for no notice. They contain, however, some points which deserve more particular comment. Sura II., the longest in the Koran, contains reference to a great variety of subjects, among which is the institution of the Fast of Ramadhân (Ramazan). On this, the ninth month of the Mahometan year, the Faithful are to fast during the day, from dawn, when there is light enough to distinguish between a white and black thread, till sunset. Certain relaxations are allowed for the sick, and those on a journey, &c. Within the prescribed hours no food or water is to pass the lips; and as the month is fixed according to the retrogressive seasons of the lunar year,[2] its occurrence during the heats of summer cause it to press with

[1] These are as follow :—113, 114, 2, 47, 57, 8, 58, 65, 98, 62, 59, 24, 63, 48, 61, 4, 3, 5, 33, 60, 66, 49, 9. *Vide* Muir, vol. ii. Appendix.

[2] Sura ix. 36, 37. Each month retrogrades eleven days, according to the solar year.

double rigour in the parched regions of Africa, Arabia, and India. Those who have dwelt among the Mahometans will bear testimony to the exemplary and patient manner in which the irksome duties of the fast are fulfilled by those whose doings are open to observation during the prescribed hours. Many, indeed, make a point of keeping it who neglect the appointed prayers. On the believer's proceedings during the night there is no restriction, as regards food, and social domestic intercourse;[1] and consequently it imposes no restraint on indulgence. The reader will not fail to notice how the fasting enjoined by Mahomet differs from the Christian ideal of abstinence. The one involves a painful duty made final and meritorious in itself, and the tendency of it is to alternate with the grossest licentiousness; the other, being merely a means to an end, is wisely left unfettered by such severe restrictions, and, shunning the observation of man, is to be associated with that godly sorrow for sin which worketh repentance.

The fast of the Ramadhân terminates with the festival of the "Eed-al-Fitr,"[2] or "breaking of the fast," kept on the first three days of the tenth month (Shawwal). It is celebrated as a season of general rejoicing and feasting. Certain prescribed religious observances are attended to, visits of congratulation made, and alms given as offerings to the poor.

The "Eed-al-Zoha,"[3] or "day of sacrifice," was established by the prophet at Medina, and was

[1] Sura ii. 181–183.
[2] Called by the Turks "Ramazam Beyram."
[3] Called by the Turks "Koorban Beyram."

grounded on the ceremonies of the Greater Pilgrimage. It is celebrated on the tenth of the month Dzul-Hijja, the last of their lunar year, and the day on which the pilgrims return from Arafat to Mina.

In the first year of his residence at Medina, Mahomet kept, with certain sacrifices, the great "Day of Atonement," in conformity with Jewish practice, but afterwards abandoned it, and substituted a festival of a similar character connected with the Meccan rites.[1] It is called "The Greater Festival," and lasts three days. On the first day the faithful should slay a victim if they can afford to do so. The wealthy slay several sheep, and distribute the flesh to the poor. Visits of congratulation and presents are made during its continuance.[2] "This feast is the great Muhammadan festival, and is observed wherever Islamism exists; and thus Muhammad, though he ignored entirely the doctrine of the Atonement, has become unwillingly a witness to the grand Christian doctrine, that 'without shedding of blood there is no remission.'"[3]

The two festivals above mentioned were established by the prophet himself; while that of the "Moharram,"—so called from its being kept on the first ten days of the first month of the Moslem year—is a Sunnat fast, but by some supposed to be alluded to in the Koran,[4] while others apply the allusion there to the "ten nights" differently. The days of this festival are considered eminently blessed, alms are given, and

[1] Muir, vol. iii. pp. 51, 52. [2] Lane, i. 232; ii. 252.

[3] "Notes on Muhammadanism," pp. 110, 111.

[4] Sura lxxxix. 1.

it is kept as a season of rejoicing. The last day—the "Ashura," is considered sacred for a variety of reasons: because that on it Noah left the ark, &c., but its greatest claim to sanctity is, that on it the martyr Hosein, grandson of the prophet, was slain in battle at the Kerbela (A.D. 680). The anniversary of this event is kept, especially by the Shias, with expressions of profound grief.[1] In memory of his death, models of his tomb, called "Tazias," are in India buried, and his name invoked. At Cairo the great mosque in which his head is supposed to rest is visited, prayers offered, and his martyrdom commemorated.[2]

Directions are given regarding the pilgrimage to the holy places,—to Mecca, "appointed a place of resort for all mankind,"[3] with the minute ceremonies to be performed by the Faithful. It is declared to be a positive "duty towards God, on those who are able to go thither,"[4] but it does not appear to be absolutely necessary to salvation, though the Sunnah makes it so.[5] The orthodox sects also differ in their interpretation of the Koran on this subject.[6] Trading is permitted during the pilgrim-

[1] The Shias however keep all the days of the Moharram as a season of lamentation, and commemorate on them the deaths of Ali and Hasan, who, as well as Hosein, are esteemed martyrs.

[2] There are certain other festivals, of which we may mention, 1. Shub-Barât, the "night of record," on which God registers the actions of the coming year, observed on the 15th of the month Shaban. 2. Bara-Wafât, the anniversary of the death of Mahomet, on the 12th of the month Rabi I.

[3] Sura ii. 119.

[4] Sura iii. 91.

[5] Sale, Pre. Dis., p. 114.

[6] Lane, "Mod. Egyp.," i. 131.

age—an astute provision which, with pious guile, combines in one solemn act the usually antagonistic pursuits of piety and profit [1]

There can be little doubt that Mahomet associated the pilgrimage to Mecca with some undefined, though real spiritual advantage. It was hallowed in his own earliest associations, venerable as the traditional place of prayer of Abraham; and having, as he imagined, been purged from all trace of idolatry, he considered that from it, "the first house assigned unto men to worship,"[2] the prayers of the pilgrim would ascend with especial acceptance to Heaven. With such views of the inherent sanctity of the spot, we need not be surprised that he included, in the ceremonial observances of his religion, the ancient rites of the pilgrimage, which were associated with the names of their ancestors, Abraham and Ishmael, and from which the grosser forms of idolatry had been swept away.

By the earnest Mahometan of the present day, the distant journey to Mecca is undertaken as a matter of obedience to the direction of his prophet, and from his belief that such visit is in itself fraught with rich blessing, apart from its effect on his will and character.[3] That such is practically believed may be gathered from the fact, that according to the Hanifees, the pilgrimage may be done by deputy, and, according to custom in Morocco, even after a person's death.

[1] Sura ii. 194. Com. St. Matt. vi. 24. [2] Sura iii. 90.

[3] Moslems dying on the Pilgrimage are, *ipso facto*, considered martyrs. Each step, too, taken by the devotee towards the Kaaba blots out a sin!

Viewed in its practical working, the visit to Mecca, so far from having any effect in spiritualizing the life, or improving the character of the devotees, exposes them, according to the testimony of an eye-witness, to the most demoralizing influences. Burckhardt states that the prevalence of indecent practices at Mecca tends in no small degree to poison the morals of the pilgrims, who have opportunity of witnessing places, the most hallowed in their faith, polluted by the grossest abominations. He also states that he has seen the Kaaba itself made the scene, at nights, of detestable proceedings, which were pursued without shame or censure. The truth indeed is, whatever Mahomet hoped from the institution, that the pilgrimage has become, or rather continues to be, nothing but a superstitious and idolatrous pageant, worthless for the purpose of true religion, and degrading in its ultimate effect on the soul.[1]

The use of wine — including all inebriating liquors—lots, and all games of chance, is absolutely forbidden. Thus, "in wine and lots . . . . there is great sin, and also things of use to men, but their sinfulness is greater than their use."[2] And, again, at a later time, and in stronger terms: "wine and lots . .

[1] To the devout and thoughtful Moslem, the ridiculous ceremonies of the Pilgrimage must be in painful contrast with the otherwise decorous externals of his faith. Undoubtedly one of the idolatrous practices of Arabia, it was retained by Mahomet, either because it suited his purpose to do so, or because he did not feel himself strong enough to abolish it, if indeed such an idea ever occurred to him.

[2] Sura ii. 216.

are an abomination of Satan; therefore avoid them, . . . by them Satan seeks to divert you from remembering God, and from prayer."[1] The use of opium, though not mentioned in the Koran, is deemed unlawful."[2]

Salvation, according to Mahomet, is to be secured by following God's direction, as contained in the Koran, by believing in the mysteries of the faith, keeping covenants, observing the appointed times of prayer, distributing alms, and having a firm assurance of the life to come, and in performing good works. Such, it is said, are directed by the Lord, and they shall prosper.[3] The joys of Paradise are to be obtained only by the rigid performance of all the observances of the faith; and the value of the believer's works are to be weighed by a hard taskmaster rather than a loving Father; the dread of whose displeasure, more than the smile of whose favour, is to be the motive principle of action. In his earlier teaching at Medina, Mahomet gave utterance to the doctrine that "Jews and Christians and Sabians, whoever believeth in God and the last day"[4] would be saved; but the general consensus of orthodox Moslems is, that this passage is entirely abrogated by a later revelation, which expressly declares that "whosoever followeth any other religion than Islam, it shall not be accepted of him, and in the next life he shall be of those who perish."[5] The faithful are repeatedly reminded that

[1] Sura v. 92, 93.

[2] Regarding the practical observance of these injunctions, *vide* Lane, "Modern Egyptians," pp. 130–136.

[3] Sura ii. 1–4. [4] Sura ii. 59. [5] Sura iii. 79.

"one soul cannot make satisfaction for another, and that no intercessor will be accepted for any man, nor shall any compensation be received."[1] In these and in other passages of a similar import the idea of an Intercessor or of any Atonement provided for man is quite repudiated.

Notwithstanding these positive assertions, the deep need of fallen humanity for an Intercessor, as a medium of approach to a holy God,—seen in every nation, and underlying all religions,—influences the practice of the majority of the followers of Islam. Mahomet is made an intercessor, and saints and imams have been established in various places, at whose tombs sacrifices are offered, and whose influence is sought as channels of approach to the All-Merciful Allah.[2]

War against infidels, as already related, is commanded; the prophet is expressly directed to stir up the faithful to its performance, and the promise is held out that superior numbers shall not avail the enemy. In the infancy of Islam it was shown to be God's will that captive prisoners should be cut off; but afterwards their ransom was made lawful.[3]

The forty-seventh chapter directs that the un-

[1] Sura ii. 45.

[2] Burton, ii. pp. 76–309. Also Lane, "Mod. Egyp.," i. pp. 79, 129, 132, 325; ii. pp. 175, 295. Also Freeman, "The Saracens," pp. 62, 71. The teaching of the ancient Hindoo faith includes the doctrine of original sin, and the necessity for regeneration; gives rules for the expiation of offences, and inculcates the belief in some divine incarnation and the need of a saviour (Monier Williams, "Indian Wisdom," pp. 146, 245, 278, 321, *et seq.*).

[3] Sura viii. 66–69.

believers are to be slaughtered till all opposition has ceased, and God's religion reign alone. They who fall in the holy war are to be accounted martyrs, and their reward is Paradise.[1] During the four sacred months,—Moharram, Rajab, Dzul Caada, and Dzul Hijja, the first, seventh, eleventh, and twelfth of the Moslem lunar year,—war may be made on infidels and on those who do not acknowledge them to be sacred, otherwise it is to cease while they last.[2] Captive women are to be reduced to slavery, and, though already married, may be taken as concubines.[3] The Faithful are forbidden to contract friendship with Jews, Christians, and unbelievers.[4]

Wilful murder is forbidden in the Koran, and its punishment, in the case of the slaughter of a believer, is declared to be "Hell fire for ever."[5] The law of retaliation is to be enforced for this crime, the free is to die for the free, the slave for the slave; but the heir of the murdered man—the avenger of blood—may commute the punishment, and "prosecute the murderer according to what is just," that is, accept a fine;[6] but he is not, on pain of retaliation, to torture his victim to death, or to exceed what is a fitting punishment.[7] Manslaughter is to be expiated by a lesser punishment—freeing a believer from captivity, paying a fine, or fasting two months. Of the punishment for theft I have already spoken.

[1] Sura xlvii. 4–7.
[2] Sura ix. 36. Sale, P. D., p. 149.
[3] Sura iv. 28.
[4] Sura v. 56.
[5] Sura iv. 95.
[6] Sura ii. 173.
[7] Sura xvii. 35. The Moslem code in this particular is much laxer than the Jewish (Numb. xxxv. 31). As to blood revenge, *vide* Lane, "Mod. Egyp.," i. 145.

In the case of testamentary documents there are to be two witnesses, just men, who, on any dispute, are to be examined apart after the evening prayer, and are to give their evidence on oath.[1] By the law of the Koran, primogeniture carries no especial privileges, but each son has an equal share in the property of the deceased, and that share is double the portion allotted to a daughter. The testator cannot, it would seem, will away from his family more than one third of his estate, the rest goes to his children, or brothers, or parents, and to his wives in certain fixed proportions. The rule is laid down that men and women ought to have a part of what their parents and kindred leave,[2] and this seems to have been worthily designed by Mahomet, to stop the common practice of the pagan Arabs, who would not allow women and children to have any inheritance, giving all the goods of the deceased to those who could go to war.[3]

Almsgiving is a duty enjoined. Alms are of two kinds, legal (Zacât), and voluntary (Sadacât), though this distinction is not always observed. Under the latter head, the prophet's fifth share of all booty taken in war is included.[4] The former, in the early days of Islam, was collected by officers especially appointed for the purpose, and amounted to about a tenth part of the increase. Alms are directed to be given of the good things which believers receive, without ostentation; they are said to be noticed by God; and, if done in secret, that

[1] Sura v. 105.

[2] Sura iv. 8–18.

[3] Lane, "Mod. Egyp.," p. 143.

[4] Muir, iv. 155.

they atone for sins, and shall have their reward.[1] The collection of the legal tithes, as at first the practice under the early Caliphs, has now generally ceased in Mahometan countries, other taxes having taken their place, and it is now left to each man's conscience to give what he will. The Caliph Omar II. (of the house of Omeya) said that prayer carried the believer half-way to God, fasting brought him to His door, and that alms gained him admission. Some pretend to give the legal alms during the first ten days of Moharram, and their charity generally takes the form of distributing food to the poor. Alms-giving is practised by many who neglect the other duties of their religion. They look upon it as involving a more personal sacrifice, as fraught with more immediate benefit, and as a certain method of securing the prayers and blessings of those whom they relieve. There are, I doubt not, many of the Faithful who do their alms in secret, worthily and acceptably, but the Christian motive for its practice is little known where Islam holds sway.

Circumcision, though as a rule practised by the Mahometans, is not a positive precept, not being mentioned in the Koran. It was practised by the Arabs before Mahomet's time, and was continued by the Faithful as an Abrahamic rite. It is not universal. Some of the Berbers of Morocco do not use it. Circumcision usually takes place between the sixth and twelfth years.[2]

[1] Sura ii. 266–275.

[2] Lane, "Mod. Egyp.," i. 82; ii. 278.

CHAPTER X.

ISLAM.

It may be proper here to enter somewhat more fully than has been done in the preceding chapters into the meaning of some of the principal terms used in the book, and to enlarge upon some of the divisions of Islam.

The religion founded by Mahomet is called "Islam,"[1] a word meaning "the entire surrender of the will to God"; its professors are called "Mussulmans,"[2]—"those who have surrendered themselves," or "Believers," as opposed to the "Rejectors" of the Divine messengers, who are named "Kafirs," or Mushrikîn,[3] that is, "those who associate, are companions or sharers, with the Deity."

Islam is sometimes divided under the two heads of Faith, and Practical Religion. I. Faith (Imân) includes a belief in one God, omnipotent, omniscient, all-merciful, the author of all good; and in Mahomet as his prophet, expressed in the formula "There is no God but God, and Mahomet is the Prophet of God." It includes, also, a belief in the authority and sufficiency of the Koran,[4] in angels, genii, and the devil, in the immortality of the soul, the resurrection,[5] the day of judgment,[6] and in

[1] Sura iii. 17. [2] Sura ii. 122. [3] Muir, ii. 147.

[4] Sura xvi. 91, and vi. 114. The word Koran (Qurân) is derived from the Arabic, Quaraa, to read, and means "the reading," or "what ought to be read." It has a variety of other names, "Al Katab," the book; "Al Moshaf," the volume; "Al Forkan," the book distinguishing between good and evil, &c.

[5] Sura xvii. 52–54. [6] Sura vii. 186, 187; lvi. 1–96.

God's absolute decree for good and evil.[1] II. Practical Religion (Dîn) consists of five observances:—(1) Recital of the Formula of Belief, (2) Prayer with Ablution, (3) Fasting, (4) Almsgiving, (5) the Pilgrimage. In the above pages I have made more particular mention of these separate articles of faith, and acts of devotion.

It will be sufficient here to repeat, though every act is supposed to be prefaced with the words, "In the name of God, the merciful, the compassionate" (Bismillah-hir-rahmān-nir-rahim), and though in some places the Koran seems to deny the meritorious efficacy of good works, that, in the belief of the orthodox, Paradise is only to be obtained by a strict performance of all the practical duties above enumerated.

The standard of Moslem orthodoxy is essentially the Koran, and to it primary reference is made; but, this being found insufficient, as Islam extended its borders, to regulate the complex, social, and political relations of the empire, and the administration of justice in civil and criminal cases, some more extended and discriminating code became necessary. The deficiency was supplied by the compilation of the "Sunnah," or "Traditional Law," which is built upon the sayings and practices of Mahomet, and, in the opinion of the orthodox, is "invested with the force of law, and with some of the authority of inspiration."[2]

The traditions appear to have remained un-

[1] Sura xxx. 29; l. 28.

[2] Muir, i. 31. The collections of these traditions are also called "Hadīs" (conf. "Notes on Muhammadanism," v. "The Traditions," p. 30).

recorded for about a century after the death of Mahomet, when they were formally collected by Omar II., and the work was continued by his successors. An incredible number of so-called "Traditions," fabricated for the purpose of upholding certain political and sectarian claims, were subsequently rejected, and the Sunnah condensed and promulgated for the guidance of the faithful. "The six standard Sunni collections were compiled exclusively under the Abbâsside caliphs, and the earliest of them partly during the reign of Al Mâmûn.[1] The four canonical collections of the Shîas were prepared somewhat later, and are incomparably less trustworthy than the former, because their paramount object is to build up the divine Imâmat, or headship of Ali and his descendants."[2]

In cases where both the Koran and the Sunnah afford no exact precept, the "Rule of Faith" in their dogmatic belief, as well as the decisions of their secular courts, is based upon the teaching of one of the four great Imâms, or founders of the orthodox sects, according as one or another of these prevails in any particular country.

These sects, though all are considered sound in fundamentals, differ in some points of law and religion, and follow the interpretation of the Koran, and the traditions of the four great doctors, Abu Hanifa, Malik, Al Shafei, and Ibn Hambal.[3] The

[1] A.D. 814-834.

[2] Muir, i. 41. The Wahabees receive the "Sunnah," which is acknowledged by the Sunnis, and call themselves, *par excellence*, "People of the Traditions."

[3] The Hanifee school which is considered the most catholic and reasonable, prevails in Turkey, Egypt, and North India. In

great Sunni sect is divided among the orthodox schools mentioned above, and is so called from its reception of the "Sunnah," as having authority concurrent with and supplementary to the Koran.[1]

In this respect it differs essentially from the "Shîas," or partisans of the house of Ali, who, adhering to their own traditions, reject the authority of the "Sunnah." These two sects, moreover, have certain observances and matters of belief peculiar to themselves, the chief of which is the Shîa doctrine, that the sovereign Imâmat, or temporal and spiritual headship over the faithful, was by divine right vested in Ali and in his descendants, through Hasan and Hosein, the children of Fatima, the daughter of the prophet. And thus the Persian Shîas add to the formula of belief, the confession, "Ali is the Caliph of God."

In Persia the Shîa doctrines prevail, and formerly so intense was sectarian hatred, that the Sunni

Cairo, the inhabitants are either Shafe-ees or Malikees. The Malikee sect is dominant in Morocco and in other parts of Africa. The Arabians and the Moslems of Southern India generally follow the teaching of Al Shafei. Very few, except in Arabia, belong to the school of Ibn Hambal. While all admit the leading dogmas of Islam, these schools condescend to dispute over unimportant trivialities, such as the correct method of ablution, the exact position at prayer, &c. Ibn Hambal was scourged by Motasem Billah, eighth Caliph of Baghdad, for asserting that the Koran was uncreated. There are also numberless sects called heterodox, being considered heretical in fundamentals (*vide* Sale, P. D., chap. viii.).

[1] Each of these sects has its "oratory," or place of prayer, round the Kaaba and within the sacred enclosure of the "Masjid-al-Haram." Each one also (except the Hambalees) has a mufti, or expounder of their particular law, at Mecca.

Mahometans paid a higher capitation tax there than the infidels. In Turkey the great majority are Sunni. In India the Shîas number about one in twenty. The Shîas, who reject this name, and call themselves "Adliyah," or the "Society of the Just," are sub-divided into a great variety of minor sects; but these, whatever their particular views, are united in asserting that the first three Caliphs, Abu Bekr, Omar, and Othman, were usurpers, who had possessed themselves of the rightful and inalienable inheritance of Ali. For this reason, too, they detest the memory of the Omeyade Caliphs, and especially Yezid, whom they accuse of the murder of the martyr Hosein. Of this more particular mention will be hereafter made.[1]

"According to the Shîas, the Muslim religion consists of a knowledge of the true Imām, or leader, and the differences amongst themselves with reference to this question have given rise to endless divisions."[2] The twelve Imāms of the Shîa sect are, 1, Ali; 2, Hasan; 3, Hosein; 4, Zain-al-Abid-Dīn, and his eight lineal descendants, the last of whom, the twelfth, was Abu Kasim, or, as he is called, Imām Mahdī.

[1] Freeman, "The Saracens," p. 227. Humayun, the "Great Mogul," when driven out of India, was obliged, on pain of death, to adopt the Shîa doctrines, by Tamasp, second "Sophi," King of Persia. Aurungzebe was Sunni, and put one of his brothers to death on the pretext that he had adopted the Shîa heresy. For an account of the Shîa sects *vide* Sale, P. D., viii. p. 75. And for the chief points of difference between them and the Sunnis, p. 178. See also "Notes on Muhammadanism," xliii., "The Shîas," p. 169.

[2] "Notes on Muhammadanism," p. 171 *et seq.*

He is supposed by them to be still alive, though concealed from public eye, and is to come again to extinguish all disputes among the true believers.

Sufi-ism.—In India and Persia, and throughout the East, there has for centuries existed a pantheistic mysticism which has developed itself chiefly in a search for metaphysical purity, for the illumination of the mind, for calmness of soul, and for the subjugation of the passions, by the exercise of painful austerities, and the adoption of an ascetic life. The adherents of this system believed that the divine nature pervaded all things, and gave its very essence and being to the soul itself, which thus sought to gain a conformity to the Supreme Being, and more and more to sever itself from the things of earth, like a wearied traveller, seeking to terminate the period of its exile from its divine original. From this pantheistic mysticism, akin to the doctrine of the Indian Vedanta, Plato is supposed to have derived the germs of some of his teaching; and from it the Mahometan Sufis[1] had their origin. The final object of the Sufi devotee is to attain to the light of Heaven, towards which he must press forward till perfect knowledge is reached in his union with God, to be consummated, after death, in absorption into the Divine Being. In this spiritual journey of the disciple there are various stages; he is led up from his natural state, through science, love (Ishaq), seclusion, knowledge, ecstacy, touch, and, lastly, union with God, to final extinction. It should

[1] A word derived by some from sūf, wool (Arabic), the material worn by the devotees, or from the Greek σοφος.

be noticed that the terms love of God, truth, &c., have, in Sufi theology, an especial and mystic meaning, very different from their usual acceptation in Christian terminology. Their chief doctrines are taught under the images of wine, love, flowing ringlets, and intoxication; and they are supposed to be thus set forth in the Anacreontic verses of Hafiz, the distinguished Sufi poet.[1]

The Wahabees derive their name from Abdul Wahab, the father of Sheikh Muhammad, their founder, who arose about the beginning of the last century, in the province of Najd, in Arabia. The object of the Wahabee movement was to sweep away all later innovations, and to return to the original purity of Islam, as based upon the exact teaching of the Koran and the example of Mahomet. The principles of the sect rapidly spread among the Arab tribes, and were adopted by the sovereign princes of Darayeh, in Najd. Impelled by religious zeal and political ambition, and allured by the prospect of plunder, the Wahabees soon acquired nearly the whole of Arabia, and menaced the neighbouring Pashaliks of Turkey, and Egypt. Mecca and Medina soon fell into their hands, the shrine was despoiled of its rich ornaments, and the pilgrim route to the Kaaba closed for some years. Early in this century (1811), Muhammad Ali, the Pasha of Egypt, at the bidding of the Sultan, set himself to check the progress of this aggressive sect; and his son Ibrahim Pasha completed the work (1818) by the total defeat of Abdallah, their leader, who was sent to Constantinople and executed. The chief seat of their power at present is in Eastern Arabia, but

[1] Conf. Hughes, "Notes on Muhammadanism," p. 162.

followers of the sect exist in most Mahometan countries. The leader of the sect in India was Syud Ahmed, born at Rai Bareli, in Oudh, in 1706.[1]

It only remains to notice the Darveshes[2] or Faqirs,[3] and it will only be possible in our limited space to glance at the principal orders, the lesser being so numerous that D'Ohsson reckons thirty-two. They "are divided into two great classes: the 'Ba-Shara' (with the law), or those who govern their conduct according to the principles of Islam; and the 'Be-Shara' (without the law), or those who do not rule their lives according to the principles of any religious creed, although they call themselves Mussulmans."[4] The former, however, only can properly be so considered. They trace their line of succession from Abu Bekr (Sadiq) and Ali-al-Murtuza, the first and fourth Caliphs, who are said to have founded the orders of faqirs. Some writers have distinguished their minor sects by their dress and religious performances; but this rule does not seem to hold, and it is impossible to become exactly acquainted with their peculiar rules and ceremonies, as, like those of the Freemasons, they are concealed from the unini-

[1] The following particulars of the Wahabee reform need only be added. They reject the decisions of the "four orthodox doctors," and the intercession of saints; they condemn the excessive reverence paid to Mahomet, and deny his mediation, until the last day. They also disapprove of the ornamenting of tombs, pilgrimages to particular shrines, offerings, &c.

[2] From the Persian "dar," a door=beggars from door to door.

[3] From the Arabic "faqir," poor, but used rather as poor in the sight of God than of men.

[4] Hughes, "Notes on Muhammadanism," p. 139.

tiated. Some of them practise the most severe austerities and mortifications.

The order which has excited most interest in Europe, being popular in Constantinople, is that of the "Maulevis," or dancing darveshes, whose ceremonies constitute one of the principal sights of that city, and have often been described by travellers and pictured by artists. Their founder was a native of Balkh, in Central Asia, and is said to have exhibited remarkable faith and miraculous power from his infancy. The darveshes or faqirs are either "Murids" (disciples) or "Murshids" (guides), and the places where the latter give their instructions are held sacred, and carefully kept free from pollution. Those faqirs who attain to great sanctity are called "Walis," and the highest rank of these is that of a "Ghaus," such as the Akhund of Swāt, on the north-west frontier of India.

The particular ceremony or act of devotion common to all classes of darveshes is the "Zikr," or repetition of the names of God in many different ways. It is a sort of physical exercise, depending upon the lungs, muscles, and patient practice of the worshipper, and would appear to a Christian the very opposite of rational devotion. There are two classes of Zikr, one which is recited aloud, and the other performed with a low voice or mentally; and each is divided into several zarbs, or stages. As an instance: the third zarb of the quiet prayer consists in repeating the words "La-il-la-ha" with each exhalation of the breath, and "Il-lal-la-ho"[1] with each inhalation; and being performed hundreds, or even thousands of times, it is most exhausting, and proportionately meritorious.

[1] Combined, these syllables make "There is no deity but God."

The meditation (Muraqaba) is usually combined with the Zikr, and is founded on favourite verses of the Koran. It must, one would suppose, form a needed rest after so fatiguing an exercise. "The most common form of Zikr is a recital of the ninety-nine names of God, for Muhammad promised those of his followers who recited them a sure entrance into paradise."[1] To assist this repetition rosaries are used, but not by the Wahabees, who count on their fingers. It has been conjectured that the Mahometans derived the rosary from the Buddhists, and that the Crusaders again took it from them (A.D. 1100). Moulvies declare that the mind is preserved from the intrusion of evil thoughts by the performance of the Zikr; but it is worthy of remark, that some of those most devoted to its use are the most immoral of men.[2]

Sufficient for the purpose of this manual has been said about the daily and periodical religious duties of the faithful; and I now pass to a brief consideration of their belief regarding the soul and body after separation. On the occurrence of death—as burial must, as a rule, take place the same day—the necessary preparations are at once begun. The body is washed, wrapped in one or two pieces of cotton cloth, and so carried to the grave, usually a vaulted chamber, with observances and attendants regulated by the wealth of the deceased.

The Mahometans believe that the soul remains with the body during the first night after burial for the purpose of being interrogated by the two angels, Munkir and Nakir. Laid on the right side,

[1] Hughes, "Notes on Muhammadanism," pp. 155.

[2] Ib., 154.

with the sightless eyes turned towards Mecca, the dead awaits the coming of the dread inquisitors. Aroused to a sitting posture and to temporary life, he answers their inquiries as to his faith in God and in his prophet regarding the "Book of Directions," the Koran, and whether or not the Kaaba was his Kibla. If the answers be unsatisfactory, they torture and beat the dead about the temples with their iron maces; if satisfactory, they give him their peace, and bid him sleep on in the protection of God. The examination in the grave is founded on tradition, and is supposed also to be twice alluded to in the Koran, though certain sects deny it altogether. Thus: "How, therefore, will it be with them (the unbelievers), when the angels shall cause them to die, and shall strike their faces and their backs."[1]

On the completion of this examination the soul is conveyed to a place called Berzakh,[2] or "the Barrier," the Hades of separate spirits, there to remain till reunited to the body. The faithful are, according to their works, in various degrees of happiness. The souls of the prophets are at once admitted to Paradise; those of martyrs dwell in the crops of green birds, which eat of the fruits and drink the waters of the happy gardens, &c.; while the souls of the wicked have a foretaste of those torments which, when reunited to their bodies, they are to suffer for ever.

The general resurrection and judgment, in which

[1] Sura xlvii. 29. See also Sura viii. 52; Sale, P. D., sec. iv.; and Lane, ii. chap. xv. At the funeral of the rich in Egypt, a sacrifice, called "the expiation," is offered, generally a buffalo, the flesh of which is given to the poor.

[2] Suras xxiii. 102; xxv. 55.

are to be included all beings, even as it appears, the brute creation,[1] will be announced by the trumpet of the angel "Israfil," when, "the earth shall shine by the light of its Lord, and the book shall be laid open, and every soul shall be fully rewarded according to what it shall have wrought. And the unbelievers shall be driven unto hell by troops,—but those who shall have feared their Lord, shall be conducted by troops towards paradise" (Sura xxxix. 67–73).

Such is a general outline of the last day, which clearly indicates a belief in individual responsibility, and that the sentence of happiness or misery is regulated according to each man's works, which are to be weighed in the just balance "that hangs over Paradise and Hell, and is capacious enough to hold both Heaven and Earth."[2] The judgment being over, the Faithful, and the "companions of the left hand," have still one final ordeal to undergo, viz., the passage of the bridge "Al Sirât," which, spanning "the deep abyss of hell," is finer than a hair, and sharper than the edge of a sword. Over it the true Moslems, headed by their prophet, will pass into Paradise, with the fleetness of the wind, whilst the wicked will fall headlong into the gulf beneath.[3] The teaching of the Koran regarding heaven and hell has already been noticed.

[1] Sura vi. 38. "There is no kind of beast on earth, nor fowl—but the same is a people like unto you—unto their Lord shall they return."

[2] Sale, P. D., p. 89. Comp. Sura xxiii. 104, 105.

[3] This myth of the bridge "Al Sirât" rests on tradition, and was taken from the Magians (conf. Sale, P. D., sec. iv.).

CHAPTER XI.

THE SPREAD OF ISLAM.

NEWS of the prophet's death soon spread among his disciples. The fiery Omar combated the assertion, and maintained that a swoon only had fallen on him, but Abu Bekr, in words of the Koran itself,[1] assured the Faithful that from the common lot of humanity there was no exemption even for the apostle of God. And so Mahomet's body was prepared for the grave, and, clad in the garments in which he died, was buried in Ayesha's chamber, beneath the spot where the angel of death had visited him.

Abu Bekr, not without some show of opposition on the part of the "Ansâr," was elected Caliph or successor of the apostle, having, as was asserted by his supporters, been virtually nominated to the office by Mahomet himself.[2]

The dignity of Caliph, it should be remembered, carried with it the supreme temporal and spiritual authority over the Faithful. Throughout

[1] Sura xxxix. 31: "Verily, thou, O Mahomet, shalt die."

[2] The Ansâr put forward Sâd, one of their number. It was thought by the partizans of Ali that his marriage with Fatima gave him an inherent right to the succession. This claim, afterwards intensified, divides to the present day the Mahometan world.

Arabia the death of the prophet was followed by a general spirit of insurrection among the Bedouin tribes, who eagerly sought to shake off their allegiance to the new faith; but in the first year of his reign, Abu Bekr succeeded not only in reducing them to obedience, but also, by the prospect of boundless plunder, and the joys of Paradise, in enlisting their numbers, and in pressing into the service of the faith the irresistible fanaticism of these children of the desert.

Under Khalid, the province of Irak was overrun, and the city of Ambar, and that of Hira with its Christian population, subjected to tribute. War was declared against Heraclius, and Syria invaded. Khalid was directed to join his troops to those of Abu-Obeida in the valley of the Jordan, and at the battle of Aiznadin the forces of the Byzantine monarchy were totally defeated. At this conjuncture Abu Bekr died, after a short reign of two years and four months, and Omar, who had been nominated to the dignity by his predecessor, was regarded as Caliph.[1]

Under the Caliph Omar (A.D. 634—643) the tide of conquest rolled on. Bostra and Damascus, Antioch and Aleppo fell and became tributary, and Syria was finally subdued. The victory of Yermouk (A.D. 636) gave the invaders entry into Palestine, and Jerusalem surrendered to the Caliph in person. Mounted on his camel, a bag of dates and a skin of

[1] Abu Bekr was a man of the purest character. His friendship for Mahomet, and unwavering belief in his mission, are a strong testimony to the sincerity of the prophet.

water by his side—ample provision for his simple wants,—he made his entry into the sacred city. Honourable terms of capitulation were granted to its inhabitants, and the provisions of the treaty faithfully observed. On mount Moriah, the site of the temple of Solomon, he obtained permission to erect "The Dome of the Rock," which, as the Mosque of Omar, bears his name to this day.

Meanwhile, the great victory of Cadesia (A.D. 636), won by his lieutenants over Yesdejird—the last of the Sassanidæ,—was followed by the capture of the capitals Ctesiphon and Seleucia; while the subsequent "victory of victories" on the plain of Nahavend finally subjected Persia to tribute or the faith. Eygpt, too, on the fall of Memphis and Alexandria (A.D. 640), was wrested from the Roman Empire by Amru, and with part of Libya incorporated with the caliphate.

Omar was the first who bore the title of "Prince of the Faithful," and though his empire extended from the Orontes to the Arabian Sea, and from the Caspian to the Nile, he affected no regal state, was the friend and companion of the beggar and the poor, and in his mud palace at Medina was ready to share his meal with the humblest brother in the faith. There is a grand simplicity, and a heroism, in the lives of these early warriors of the crescent which irresistibly strikes the imagination, and places them in noble contrast with the cruel and effeminate despots who soon succeeded them. Omar perished by the hand of a Persian slave (A.D. 643), and with him the golden age of the undivided caliphate begins to pass away. Before his death he confided to six of the chiefs at Medina the selection of a successor, and the choice fell on Othman, who had married in succession two of the daughters of the prophet.

Ali was thus again passed over, but loyally gave in his adherence to the new Caliph, whose lieutenants continued to extend and consolidate the empire. The victorious arms of the Arabs were carried to the pillars of Hercules, though the north coast of Africa was not totally subdued for sixty years. The coasts of Andalusia were menaced, Cyprus (A.D. 647) and Rhodes (A.D. 652) subdued, and Nubia made tributary; while eastward the great province of Khorassan, which had been invaded by Omar, with its towns of Balkh and Nisabor, was added to the empire of the Caliph.

Compared with Abu Bekr and Omar, simple and zealous apostles of the faith, the character of Othman showed, in many respects, an inferiority which weakened his influence, and eventually hastened his death. Though brave and liberal, the weight of seventy years pressed upon him, and his facile disposition inclined him to lend too favourable an ear to the solicitations of his near relations and personal friends, and this to the prejudice of those whose services gave them the strongest claim to the important offices of the State. Discontent at the favouritism which prevailed became general, rival and ambitious chiefs spread the disaffection, and the tumults which arose ended in the murder of the aged Caliph (A.D. 654). With his violent death begins that long story of bloodshed and treachery which henceforth stains the history of Islam; and which, arising from political ambition, and theological disputes regarding *de jure* and *de facto* rights, is to this day illustrated by the bitterest sectarian feelings, and not unfrequently by deeds of blood.

The apparently unanimous voice of the people of Medina raised to the throne, Ali, the nearest relative, and the son-in-law of the Prophet. A large section, indeed, of Mahometans, the Shîas, as I have above stated, consider that in him and in his sons Hasan and Hosein — the sole descendants of the Prophet—was vested from the first a divine and inalienable right to the spiritual and temporal leadership of the Faithful. They thus look upon the first three Caliphs as usurpers. The legitimate succession of these three princes is upheld by the great Sunni sect, who differ from their Shîa opponents in this, and in other particulars of a more purely doctrinal nature. The Sunnis assert that Mahomet never intended, and in reality took no steps, to establish any hereditary right in his descendants, but left to the Faithful the free choice of their prince and Imām.

The chivalrous Ali (A.D. 654), the Bayard of the faith, had at length reached the goal of his ambition, but his short reign was an uninterrupted scene of civil war, which stopped the conquests begun by his predecessors, and terminated only with his untimely death at the assassin's hand. Amru, Governor of Egypt, Ayesha, the "Mother of the Faithful," and Muavia, who ruled in Syria, continued his bitter and successful opponents to the end.

Muavia, the son of Abu-Sofian and of Hind

who owed his fortune and position to Othman, refused to acknowledge Ali as lawful Caliph, called him a "man of blood," and justified his own defection under the pretext that Ali had instigated the murder of his predecessor. He further announced his intention of avenging the innocent blood which had been shed, and for this purpose usurped the independent government of the province in which he commanded. He was the first Caliph of the dynasty of the Omeyades, so called from the name of his ancestor, Omeya, the son of Abd-Shams. Fourteen princes of this house reigned at Damascus during the next hundred years (A.D. 654–752); till by the employment of arts similar to those they had used against the family of Ali, their power was undermined, their race hunted down and nearly exterminated, and in their place the great house of the Abbassides became rulers of the Eastern caliphate from their seat at Baghdad. Of the Omeyades one prince only, Abd-al-Rahman, escaped the proscription, and, making his way to Spain, founded the dynasty which continued for three centuries at Cordova (A.D. 756–1038).

On the assassination of Ali (A.D. 660), his son Hasan was acknowledged Caliph in Arabia, and in the province of Babylonia,[1] but his pacific disposition induced him, after six months, to surrender his sovereign rights to Muavia, who already reigned in Syria and Egypt. Hasan retired into private life at Medina, employing his time in prayer and almsgiving, and was subsequently poisoned by his wife at the

[1] Irak-Arabi.

instigation of the tyrant whom his resignation had confirmed on the throne.

Muavia died in A.D. 679, and was succeeded by his son, Yezid. The latter unsuccessfully laid siege to Constantinople, but extended his victories through Khorassan and Turkestan. The cities of Mecca and Medina had not, however, been consulted regarding the succession of Yezid, and encouraged the general disaffection against him. Hosein, the second son of Ali, was induced, especially by his adherents at Cufa, to raise the standard of revolt, and assert his sacred and inalienable right to the sovereign Imamat over the Faithful.

There is no event in history more mournful than the story of the martyrdom of the sainted Hosein.[1] Overtaken on his way from Mecca to join his adherents on the Euphrates, he was surrounded and perished with seventy-two of his nearest relatives. The Shîa sect, which pays to Ali and his sons honours not inferior to those given to Mahomet, detests the name of Yezid, keeps, with demonstrations of passionate grief, the festival of Hosein's death, and has made his tomb at the Kerbela a place of pilgrimage hardly inferior to Mecca.[2]

[1] Conf. Macaulay, "Life of Clive"; Freeman, "The Saracens," p. 89, *et seq.*

[2] The head of Hosein was sent to Damascus and interred in succession there and at Ascalon. Finally, it was taken to Cairo by the Fatimite Caliphs, and is reported to rest in the Mosque of the Hasanayn's. At the tomb of Fatima, in El Bakia, her sons are spoken of as "the two moons, the two pearls, the two princes of the youth of paradise." The succession of the twelve Imāms or Pontiffs of the Mahometan Church is continued through Ali, surnamed "Zayn-el-Abidin, the sole of the twelve children

It was during the reign of Valid I. (A.D. 705–716), the eldest of the four sons of Abd-al-Malik, who in succession became Caliphs of Damascus, that the empire attained its greatest extent. Its northward boundaries were Galatia and Georgia. Eastward, Transoxiana received the Mahometan law, "and the germ was planted which was to grow up into the imperial forms of the grand Turk and the great Mogul."[1] In the same year that saw the overthrow of the Gothic monarchy in Spain, the valley of the Indus submitted to the Moslem arms, and the power of the Caliph continued there to the middle of the eighth century. In the west, under Tarik, the Arabs crossed the straits from Ceuta (A.D. 710), and at Xeres, on the Guadalete, overthrew Roderic, the last of the Visigothic kings. In rapid succession Cordova and Toledo, Seville and Valentia, Saragossa and the Balearic Isles fell, and with the exception of the fastnesses of the Asturias the whole of Spain submitted to the Moors. Such names as Tarifa, Algeciras, and Gibraltar, still bear testimony to their former dominion there. Their rule, though necessarily degrading, was equitable, and the fullest religious toleration was granted. The Jews, in particular, were freed from the cruel persecutions to which they had been subject under Christian rule.[2]

of Hosein, who survived the fatal field of Kerbela" (Burton, ii. pp. 91, 257. Cf. Lane, "Mod. Egyp.," i. 291 *et seq.* 324. Also regarding the ceremonies at Cairo of the "Yom Ashoora," cf. vol. ii. p. 168).

[1] Freeman, "The Saracens," p. 106.

[2] Subsequently separate and independent kingdoms were formed at Seville, Saragossa, Valentia, and Toledo. Weakened

Thus the empire founded by the camel-driver of Mecca—the prophet of Islam—had from his humble dwelling at Medina, in less than a century, extended throughout Arabia, Syria, and Egypt, along the coast of Mauritania far into the interior of Africa, and included within its embrace Spain and part of Gaul. Eastward, Persia and Scinde had been subdued, and Transoxiana invaded, and thus the sovereign will of the Commander of the Faithful gave law from the Indus to the Atlantic. But this greatness was not to last. The immense empire contained within itself the seeds of its own dissolution, soon to germinate amidst the ambition of rival princes and the fury of contending sects. The Omeyade dynasty was, as above mentioned, supplanted by that of the house of Abbas, which, during five centuries (A.D. 752—1258) gave thirty-seven real or nominal rulers to the Eastern caliphate.

Abu Giafar, surnamed Al-Manzor, fixed the seat of his power at the new capital of Baghdad. With him the golden age of his dynasty begins. His court became the resort of the learned, and the worthy rival of Cordova in science, literature, and art. The tales of the "Arabian Nights" have made the names of Haroun-al-Raschid, fifth Caliph, and his royal spouse Zobeide, familiar to us as household words. From the reigns of his sons Al Amin, Al Mâmûn, and Al Motassem, the glory of their house begins to fade away. The ambition of the

thus by internal division, the Moors had to acknowledge the supremacy of the Castilian kings (1246), and finally confined to the kingdom of Grenada, were driven from Spain (1491).

Shîa, and other contending sects, and the insolence of the Turkish mercenaries, whom the Caliphs had taken into their pay, introduced universal anarchy, and caused the ruin of the state.

It is about the middle of the sixth century that history first makes mention of the Turks, whose original haunts were the plains of Central Asia, from the Oxus to the Arctic Circle, and from the borders of China to the Caspian Sea. Their western territories being overrun by the Arabs, they embraced the religion of their conquerors, and subsequently composed the body-guard of the Caliphs. In process of time the chiefs of this barbarous soldiery, like the Prætorians at Rome, and the Janizaries of Stamboul, arrogated to themselves the most important offices in the state, left to their sovereign only a nominal authority, and, during the height of their usurpation, subjected him to indignity, cruelty, and death.

Harassed thus by civil disorder and sectarian violence, deprived of all power, and often of personal freedom by the chiefs whom he had invited to rid him of his domestic oppressors, the Caliph was unable to check the usurpations of those who, in his name, ruled the provinces of the empire, and whose ambition it was to become the founders of separate and independent dynasties. Thus province after province was lost, and in the end Baghdad, which had been a prey to the raging factions of Sunni and Shîa, fell into the hands of the Mogul Hologu, whom the Seyuds of the house of Ali had incited against their sovereign, and the unfortunate Mostadhem Billah, the last Caliph of his race, was put to a cruel death.[1]

But the Turks were destined to play a more important part in other lands, for history undoubtedly proves that the Mahometan conquests would never have spread so far had they not been aided by the vast multitudes of Tartars and Moguls, who lent to Islam their numbers and the enthusiastic heroism of their arms. Without the religion of the prophet to give these wandering hordes a common bond of union, they might still have remained buried in the depths of their primeval solitudes, and never have showed their victorious arms on the Bosphorus and the Danube.

Othman (the ancestor of the reigning dynasty at Constantinople) was the son of Ortogrul, and grandson of a Turkish emir, who, early in the thirteenth century, and on the approach of the Mogul Ghengiz Khan, left his home in Khorassan in search of some safer settlement in Asia Minor. On the march he perished in the Euphrates, but Ortogrul obtained from the Seljuc Sultan of Iconium settlements for his followers in the ancient province of Phrygia. His son, Othman, extended his possessions chiefly at the expense of the Greek emperor, and in 1299, on the death of his patron, the ruler of Iconium, assumed the title of Sultan. A succession of ten great princes, who reigned over the

[1] A.D. 1258. Consult Freeman, "The Saracens," pp. 123–160. D'Herbelôt, *voc.* Khalifat, iii. p. 455. The power of Radhi Billah, 20th Caliph, did not extend beyond the walls of Baghdad.

Ottoman Turks, widely extended their territories, and raised their military power to the first rank in Europe.

In 1328 the seat of the monarchy was fixed at Brussa, under the shadow of Mount Olympus, and Asia Minor was conquered to the Hellespont. Solyman I. first invaded Europe (1355), and Amurath I. took Adrianople (1360), made it his capital, and soon after Macedonia, Albania, and Servia were subdued. Bajazet, his successor (1389), came in contact with the Christians in central Asia, and defeated Sigismond, the king of Bohemia and Hungary, at the great battle of Nicopolis (1396). The onward course of Bajazet was checked by the Mogul Timur, who invaded Asia Minor, and defeated him at the battle of Ancyra (1402). In 1415 Muhammad I. invaded Bavaria, and conquered the Venetians at Salonica. Though the progress of Amurath II. was arrested by the fortress of Belgrade on the Danube, and by the valour of Scanderbeg in Epirus, he defeated the Christians at Varna (1444). On the 29th May, 1453, Muhammad II. overpowered Constantinople, the last bulwark of the Christians in the East, and the noble Constantine IX, the last of the race of Paleologus, buried himself under the ruins of the city he could not save. Next followed the conquest of the Morea, and Epirus (1465), and Bosnia and Trebizond were added to his empire. For the next fifty years the Ottoman arms were the terror of Europe.

Selim I in 1517, conquered Syria and Palestine and defeated the Mamelook-sultan of Egypt. On his return to Constantinople he brought with him

Motavakkel Billah, the last titular Caliph of the family of Abbas, whom he found at Cairo. From this descendant of Dahir Billah—thirty-fifth Caliph of Baghdad—Selim "procured the cession of his claims, and obtained the right to deem himself the Shadow of God upon earth. Since then the Ottoman Padishah has been held to inherit the rights of Omar and Haroun,"[1] and to be the legitimate Commander of the Faithful, and as such possessed of plenary temporal and spiritual authority over the followers of Mahomet.[2] Solyman II, the Magnificent, took Rhodes from the knights of St. John (1522), and on the field of Mohacz (1526) subdued half of Hungary. Central Europe was threatened, and in terror, until the progress of the Moslems was checked before the walls of Vienna (1529).

From the Persians the city and territory of Baghdad were wrested; Moldavia was made tributary, and the Ottoman fleets swept the Mediterranean. The power of the Ottoman Turks had now reached its culminating point. External conquest had hitherto supplied the sinews of war; but having systematically neglected any attempt to develope the boundless resources of its vast empire, the nation has continued ever since to sink lower and lower. While surrounding Christian states have rapidly progressed, the Turks

[1] Freeman, "The Saracens," p. 158. Also D'Herbelôt's account of Mostanser Billah.

[2] It should be added that the Persian Shias repudiate these claims. The Moors also refuse to acknowledge the spiritual supremacy of the Sultan of Turkey, their own sovereign claiming to inherit the title of Caliph from the Cordovan princes.

have on the other hand remained absolutely opposed to change and reform; and in addition, the rapacity of their Sultans, carried out and imitated by extortionate pachas, has reduced the country to its present deplorable state.

A blind belief in inevitable fate, fostered by the national faith, has been a fertile source of evil. Its natural antagonism to liberty of thought and action, and to political progress, has destroyed all true national life, and has rendered reform next to impossible, and made the future hopeless. That the subjugation of alien peoples brought with it any corresponding duties to the conquered, involving the spread of true civilization, good government, and the cultivation of the peaceful arts, seems to have found no place in the thoughts of the Turks.

Centuries of despotism, with maladministration on every hand, bigoted persecution of its Christian peoples, and oppression of its co-religionists, whose cries were never allowed to disturb the torpid repose of their tyrants, have been followed by their natural and inevitable results. Instead of founding the fabric of the nation's life upon the love of a contented and loyal people, Turkey has systematically oppressed and degraded its subjects, and national dishonesty has been followed by national bankruptcy. Its bigotry, tyranny, and brutal vice have left it without friends at home, and without sympathy from abroad; and though the jealousy of rival states may for a time postpone its fall, there can be little doubt that the time must come when the Mahometan rule will be swept from those fair regions in Europe, which have for centuries been blighted by its presence.

The truth, indeed, is that so long as Mahometans are true to their own creed, so long will it be impossible for them, when they are the governing power, to grant perfect equality to their subjects of other creeds, or, when they are subjects, to render loyal and hearty obedience to a sovereign professing any antagonistic faith. For it is manifestly preposterous for them to profess obedience to, and act contrary to the whole spirit, and to the very letter of their "Book of Directions," the Koran, in which it is laid down that the unbelievers are to be held under tribute, and the Christians to be reduced low.[1]

I have above related how during the reign of Valid I, of Damascus, the province of Scinde was included in the caliphate, and how in the year A.D. 750 the invaders were driven out by the Rajpoots. For two hundred and fifty years India was free from Moslem attack. During this period, in the provinces of the crumbling caliphate, numerous dynasties, chiefly of Tartar blood, had successively established themselves westward of the Soliman range, and soon began to lend their hardy valour to the dissemination of their adopted faith.

In Afghanistan Sebuktegin, once a Turkish slave, founded a vigorous government at Ghuznee, and defeated the Hindoo Rajah of Lahore, who was the first to begin hostilities. His son Mahmoud made those famous incursions into India which are cele-

[1] Sura ix. 29.

brated in the history of that country, and annexed the Punjaub to his kingdom. Driven from their capital in Afghanistan by the Ghorian princes, the Ghuznevide dynasty lingered on for some time in their Indian possessions, till swept away by other powerful invaders (A.D. 1184).

Under a succession of Pathan princes, who rose to power with the usual circumstances of treachery and murder, the Mahometans established themselves as the dominant power in Hindustan, and penetrated into the Deccan.[1] Though the desolating wave of Mogul invasion had only swept across the north of India under Timur (1398), his descendant Baber subsequently (1526) seated himself on the throne of Delhi, in right of a pretended conquest of his great ancestor.

Under the descendants of Baber, from Akbar to Arungzebe (1556—1707), the empire of the Great Mogul reached its highest power, but during the reigns of their feeble successors it rapidly declined. The plunder of Delhi by Nadir Shah (1738) was a fatal blow to the power of the Great Mogul. It taught the hardy tribes of Rajpoots, Rohillas, Sikhs, Mahrattas, and the Mahometan viceroys themselves, the weakness of the central power, and all sought to enrich themselves at the expense of their sovereign.[2] Alternately a puppet in the hands of these nominal subjects,

[1] The Deccan was invaded and subdued by Alla-ul-Din, of the Khilji dynasty, A.D. 1295-1317.

[2] Powerful Mahometan dynasties rose from time to time in India, Kulberga (1351), Bejapore (1489), Moorshedabad, Hyderabad, in the Deccan (1717), and in Oudh and Mysore (1760).

the wretched prince was exposed to extortion, indignity, and cruelty,[1] till at length the fallen heir of Timur found a quiet asylum with the English, whom in after years his descendant sought to destroy. With the recapture of Delhi from the mutineers in 1858, the phantom power of the Great Mogul came to an end.

Unlike Hindooism, the faith of Mahomet is essentially a missionary religion, and successive Afghan, Persian, and Mogul princes have, by promise of material advantages, successfully allured converts to the faith. Freedom from the fetters of caste, and the social elevation which accompanied the adoption of Islam, induced numbers of Hindoos, chiefly of the lower classes, to adopt the ruling religion.

Eastward of India the Mahometan faith has spread among the Malays, a people of Asia who have adopted the religion and alphabet of the Arabians, and intermarried with them, so that they have become separated from the original stock, and form a distinct nation. The first missionaries of Islam reached Malacca and Sumatra in the fourteenth century, and their teaching spread to Java and the Celebes a century later. The Malays appear first in the thirteenth century in the peninsula of Malacca, where they built a town of the same name, and they subsequently spread into Sumatra, the Philippines, the Moluccas, &c. Their supremacy in these regions has passed away, chiefly through the working of the feudal system, which has divided them into number-

[1] The Emperor Farokshir (1715–1719) was assassinated; Ahmed Shah (1748–1754) was blinded and deposed; and Alumgir II. (1754–1759) deposed and murdered.

less independent peoples, and through the successful commercial rivalry of the English and Dutch. In addition to the Koran they have various local laws. Slavery is universal among them, and also the use of opium. Here, as elsewhere, the existence of Islam has utterly failed to raise the nation in a moral point of view, and either makes no effort, or is powerless, to mend the licentiousness of manners which universally abounds.

The Mahometan faith is thus prevalent from Morocco along the north coast of Africa, and southward irregularly to the equator. It dominates in Egypt and the Turkish empire, in Arabia, Persia, and Turkestan, is powerfully represented in India, and among the Malays, and has found a footing in China. Moreover, we are informed that missionary efforts for its propagation are succeeding in various parts.[1]

Assuming the population of the world to be in round numbers 1,300 millions, this total, distributed according to religious creeds, is probably as follows:—There are 490 millions of Buddhists, and the disciples of Confucius and Taoists; Christians 360 millions, Mahometans 100 millions, other beliefs 165 millions.[2] Of the 100 millions professing Islam there are in India alone some 41 millions, subjects of the Queen of England, who is thus ruler over the largest Mahometan population in the world. That these subjects are a source of strength to the Empire few will be disposed to assert, for, in face of the express directions of the prophet, loyalty becomes a

[1] Bosworth Smith, "Muhammad," pp. 25-42.

[2] Monier Williams, "Indian Wisdom," p. xxxv. note.

difficulty, which is doubtless conscientiously felt by many devout Moslems.

As I have before said, they are commanded to lay the unbeliever under tribute, and they cannot easily reconcile with this the duty of paying tribute to any Cæsar whom they regard as an infidel. To those who have no wish to be loyal, a divine justification of their acts is always welcome. Whatever may be the political conjunctions put forward as necessary to justify a crescentade or holy war for the faith, it cannot be denied that the normal condition of Islam is one of missionary aggression by the sword.

The conditions necessary to render a "Jihād" or religious war lawful have been variously interpreted by the different sects. The solution of the question seems principally to depend on whether the country in which the Moslems are subjects, is "Dar-ul-Harb," the land of enmity, or "Dar-ul-Islam," the land of Islam. Another condition has been judged by the Sunnis, necessary before the publication of a Jihād, viz., that there should be a probability of victory to their arms. The Shîas also add to this, that the armies of the Crescent must be led by the rightful Imâm.

CHAPTER XII.

CONCLUSION.

In the foregoing chapters I have attempted to present as comprehensive an account as my limits would allow of Mahomet's life and work, and now must leave to the intelligent reader the task of forming his independent opinion, of the motives which influenced his words and his deeds, and of the true value of the system he has given to the world. Towards this object the following remarks may be permitted.

Though the life and work of the prophet have in many respects so much in common, it may be found possible to judge, according to a different standard, the man and the system which he founded. The one was human, the other claims to be divine; the one acknowledges himself encompassed with the sins and errors of humanity, the other asserts its title to be the pure word of God; the one had at length to yield to the summons of the angel of death, the other claims to endure for ever as a direction and blessing to all mankind.

Mahomet arose in a barbarous country, and with no human aid so great as his own indomitable will abolished the outward expression of a cherished idolatry in his native land, bowed to himself the hearts of his countrymen, and finally gave to the world that creed which has exercised so tremendous an influence on its destiny. In the man, no one can fail to see elements of power and human greatness, which compel our wonder, if not our admiration; but in that Islam which he founded, history recognizes, in its ultimate effects, one of the greatest evils which have afflicted humanity, arising both from its hostility to the purer faith of Christianity, and also from its essential antagonism to progress, civilization, and the truth.

Judged by the smallness of the means at his disposal, and the extent and permanence of the work he accomplished, no name in the world's story shines with a more specious lustre than that of the prophet of Mecca. To the impulse which he gave, numberless dynasties have owed their existence, fair cities and stately palaces and temples have arisen, and wide provinces become obedient to the faith. And beyond all this, his words[1] have governed the belief of generations, been accepted as their rule in life and their certain guide to the world to come. At a thousand shrines the voices of the Faithful invoke blessing on him, whom they esteem the very prophet of God, the seal of the Apostles, now passed into the highest heaven as their intercessor with the All-merciful Allah.[2] Judged by the standard of human renown, the glory of what mortal can compare with his?

Attempts have been made to show that Mahomet was a true benefactor to his own countrymen. It is urged that in place of the gross idol-worship which existed, he gave to Arabia a purer

[1] It is to be remembered that in the belief of *all* the sects, Sunnis, Shîas, and Wahabees, the words and example of Mahomet are considered binding on the true believer.

[2] The Sunnis believe that their prophet has *already* received permission from God to intercede for them. The Wahabees are of opinion that this permission will not be granted till the last (day conf. Hughes, "Muhammadanism," p. 179).

faith; and we are told that incest, and infanticide, and every trace of idolatry vanished before his burning words.[1] That he did through evil and good report, under mockery and persecution, persevere with unfaltering steps in winning his countrymen to a better life and a more spiritual belief, no one can deny, and for this all honour is due to him who dwelt in a light so much brighter than the thick darkness around.

Yet, while forming a correct judgment of the moral condition of Arabia at the time when he arose, and estimating at their true value the benefits he conferred, we must not neglect to keep before our eyes the clear distinction which exists between evil and degrading practices, which are open to reform, and an imperfect, if not vicious law, intended to be the permanent standard of good and evil. The former can be successfully attacked by the influence of better example, and will disappear before a truer and higher civilization; but an evil code of ethics, enjoined by the national faith, and accepted, by its appeal to a divine origin, as the final and irrevocable standard of morality, presents an insuperable barrier to the regeneration and progress of a nation. Yet such is the position which the Koran has taken. No force can abrogate its teaching or modify its stern dogmas; not all the waters of old ocean can wash from the "Preserved Book" those revelations which degrade one-half of our humanity—woman kind,[2]

[1] Though he did, in some respects, ameliorate the condition of women and children as regards inheritances, &c., Sir W. Muir's opinion is, that woman "possessed more freedom, and exercised a healthier and more legitimate influence under the pre-existing institutions of Arabia" (Life of Mahomet, iii. 305).

[2] Sallust has the following remarks regarding the polygamy

which give their sanction to slavery, and exclude all hope of advancement in morals and in law.

However much, under the then degraded condition of Arabia, the code of Mahomet was a gift of value, and however much it may have succeeded in banishing those fiercer vices which naturally accompany ignorance and barbarism, still can it be forgotten at how dear a price the boon was acquired? In the place of temporary and remediable evils, which were honoured in the observance only, and did not seek justification by any divine sanction, the nation was delivered captive to the guidance of an unchangeable law, which, whatever the excellence of some of its precepts, poisons domestic life, stifles honest inquiry, crushes the right of private judgment, has hitherto been found, and is essentially, incompatible with constitutional freedom, and has been followed by that train of national degradation and evil which the story of the past and the example of the present show to be the constant, and it would seem the inevitable, attendants wherever Islam holds sway. History indeed but too truly records that the faith of Mahomet is altogether powerless to ennoble or to regenerate a nation. The partial and specious reforms which it may effect are vitiated by the fact that they serve to exclude the highest; and as the inner life of families, the whole tone of society, and the intellectual and moral standard of a people depend on the principles

which obtained amongst the ancient Moors and Numidians:—"Singuli pro opibus, quisque quam plurimas uxores; denas alii . . . . Ita animus multitudine distrahitur; nullam pro socia obtinet: *pariter omnes viles sunt*" (De Bello Jugurth.).

diffused by the ruling religion, it seems, from past experience, hopeless to expect that Islam will ever cease to be, what it has hitherto proved, the most formidable obstacle to the dawn of a progressive and enlightened civilization.

The question of the imposture of Mahomet is one which may best be left to the candid reader, who, from the records of his life, will judge how far he has laid himself open to so grave an imputation. That he was the impostor pictured by some writers is refuted alike by his unwavering belief in the truth of his own mission, by the loyalty and unshaken confidence of his companions, who had ample opportunities of forming a right estimate of his sincerity, and finally, by the magnitude of the task which he brought to so successful an issue. No impostor, it may safely be said, could have accomplished so mighty a work. No one unsupported by a living faith in the reality of his commission, in the goodness of his cause, could have maintained the same consistent attitude through long years of adverse fortune, alike in the day of victory and the hour of defeat, in the plenitude of his power and at the moment of death.

There were indeed times, in his later career at Medina, when it is impossible to avoid the belief that his religious enthusiasm degenerated into culpable self-deception, and the idea of a divine impulse obscured the view of his own substantial imposture.[1] His early career at Mecca was eminently pure and

[1] The affair of Zeinab, of Mary the Copt, and of his especial marital privileges, detailed in the Koran, are here referred to. On this subject, conf. "Christianity and the Religions of India' (Kennedy), pp. 214–218.

decorous, and gained him well-deserved esteem; and however much his opponents scoffed at the man "whose conversation was about heaven," none could cast in his teeth any charge of depravity. That there was, amidst much that was noble and great, an active moral declension in his character when tried in the furnace of success, it would be vain to deny. But now he has passed away, with all his weakness and frailties, and all his power, his lofty claims and aspirations, his earth-born passions and the secret motives which influenced him, and may well be left to the righteous judgment of that day when the secrets of all hearts will be revealed, and when it will be known "who are the Lord's, and who is holy."

Regarding the system which he inaugurated, I offer the following remarks. The view which we take of Mahometanism will much depend on our assurance of the truth of Christianity in its full and divine meaning. Apply this test to all who have written on the subject, and it will, I venture to think, substantially account for their varying estimate of Islam. Much too, I need hardly say, will depend on our belief in the Atonement by the death of Christ, as the means provided by God for the redemption of mankind; for in this, as the foundation of our hope, does Christianity differ essentially from the scheme devised by the prophet of Mecca.

The Koran, as above explained, however much its followers may have departed from its teaching, repudiates the idea of any vicarious sacrifice for sin, teaches expressly that each soul must account for itself to God, and denying the truth of the Christian redemption, lays upon each individual the task of atoning for his own sin, of securing pardon, and of rendering himself meet for admission to Paradise. Self-righteousness, the merit of good works, and of a rigid attention to the prescribed formularies and ceremonies of their faith, with God's mercy to supply any possible deficiency, these constitute the scheme of salvation prescribed in Islam. It will be enough to point out how fundamentally this differs from the Christian plan, which, repudiating the merit of the believer's works as in themselves propitiatory, offers the sacrifice of Christ as at once vindicating the demands of justice, fulfilling God's gracious intention towards all mankind, and giving to the sinner, through faith, the comforting assurance of pardon and reconciliation.[1]

While recognizing, then, how fundamentally Christianity and Islam differ in the plan they propose for the reconciliation of man with God, it will be well to remember that the one is the eternal purpose of our merciful and all-wise Creator, the other is the natural outcome of the human heart, which clings to the belief that it can do something to help itself and propitiate an offended judge, to whose mercy it looks to effect what is lacking, and to secure its admission to future beatitude.

[1] In conversation on this subject with a rigid Mahometan, he assured me that *they* had a redeemer,—that the martyr Hosein died for them at the Kerbela! The Shîas of India represent the deaths of both Hosein and Hasan as expiatory for the sins of men. Hasan was poisoned by his wife at the instigation of Muavia I.

That this is the practical religion of all, and even of some professing Christians, who prefer the promptings of reason to the teaching of revelation, few will deny; nor can the fact be hidden that the tendency of all spiritual faiths has been thus to degenerate; for the human heart is naturally prone to seek, by outward acts, to buy acceptance with the being it adores.

The merit of good works once admitted, other aids to faith, and new means of propitiating heaven are quickly found, and seasons and months and days, nay, particular spots, are believed to have their special efficacy in bearing aloft with acceptance the prayers of the faithful. While the Gospel prescribes for the believer's guidance pure and ennobling principles of action, the Koran, with retrogressive legislation, imposes upon those who receive it the galling fetters of a burdensome ritual; toilsome pilgrimages, severe fastings, ablutions, and the mechanical observance of the minutiæ of his faith, are substituted for purity of life; and the divorce of morality and religion soon becomes complete.

I need hardly remind the reader how important a place certain months and days and places occupy in Mahomet's scheme, and how necessary they are as adjuncts to the due performance of the ceremonies. The prophet of Mecca, whose professed mission was the extirpation of idolatry, could recognize its existence only in its grosser forms; and so subtle is its poison, has himself hopelessly fallen into the very sin he so vehemently assails. Thus his pilgrimage to the "Holy House" has especial efficacy if performed under the light of one particular moon;[1] the prayers of the faithful, to reach the ear of Allah, must be directed towards the one Kibla of their faith;[2] and their fasting is then fraught with peculiar merit if performed during the month in which the Koran descended from heaven.[3]

The rapid spread and the permanence of Islam are appealed to by Mahometans as certain proofs of its divine origin. While repudiating the validity of this deduction, it must be conceded that it presents enough to satisfy some spiritual want, and clearly points out that its tenets must have been found congenial to the peoples, who, in rapid succession adopted, and still hold to the observances it enjoins, and the licence it allows. "The causes of this new religion's rapid progress are not difficult to be discovered; Mahomet's law itself was admirably adapted to the natural disposition of man, but especially to the manners, opinions, and vices prevalent among the people of the East; for it was extremely simple, proposing few things to be believed; nor did it enjoin many and difficult duties to be performed, or such as laid severe restraints on the propensities."[4]

If to the above causes we add the powerful argument of the sword, and the wealth and honours which conquest yielded, we shall have ample reasons to account for the triumph of the crescent over the cross in those regions where, in dogma and in practice, a sensuous idolatry and relic worship called itself by

[1] Sura ii. 192. [2] Sura ii. 139. [3] Sura ii. 118.

[4] Mosheim's Eccl. Hist., book ii. chap. iii. p. 73.

the name of Christ, and for the extension to distant lands of the arms and faith of Islam. In the religious history of man, indeed, nothing is more obvious than that he has bent his strongest efforts to gain the sanction of religion for those vices to which he is naturally addicted; and this fact will be found to be the key to the corruption of all true, and to the invention of all false religions.

Regarding its aggressive action at the present day, the missionaries of Islam (to whose success in various parts a recent writer refers in terms of undisguised exultation [1]) act upon principles, the efficacy of which should awaken no wonder. Converts are expected to use only the prescribed formula of the faith, to acknowledge one God, and Mahomet as His Prophet; no examination into the nature and ground of their belief is held, outward conformity only is demanded, and time and habit are left to complete the work. No immediate repudiation of old prejudices is required, no intelligent knowledge of their new creed necessary. The worship of visible idols alone is to be abandoned; but whether the convert know anything of his newly-adopted faith, or whether it serve to produce any practical effect on the will and character, are questions altogether foreign to the object in view. Considering that social elevation follows in the wake of Islam, especially in the case of converts from the ranks of paganism, and that no real sacrifice is demanded, it will cause no wonder that it makes its way where the positive prohibitions of Christianity, and its stern demands for the fruits of a holy and religious life fail to win acceptance.

[1] Bosworth Smith, "Muhammad," p. 40.

In proposing self-righteousness as the means of salvation, Islam is admirably adapted to flatter the pride of man, and in this particular especially is it antagonistic to Christianity, which, excluding the merit of man's works, calls for inward holiness, not outside form, and summons the humble, contrite sinner in deep abasement to the foot of the cross as his only hope of pardon, his only source of peace. How difficult a task lies before the herald of the Gospel in proclaiming such an invitation to the self-righteous follower of the prophet need hardly be told. To him the reception of Christianity is compatible alone with the entire repudiation of his revered Koran; which, though professing to be a continuation of the Old and New Testament revelations, utterly destroys the very foundations of the Christian faith.

As the inner power and meaning of a religion is dead and barren, in such proportion do outward forms and ritualistic practices offer themselves as specious substitutes, and come to take the place of that inner life which alone represents the fruits of true religion. The exact ritual and formal observances of Islam have carried with them their own inevitable Nemesis, and thus we find that in the worship of the Faithful formalism and indifference, pedantic scrupulosity and positive disbelief flourish side by side. The minutest change of posture in prayer, the displacement of a single genuflexion, would call for much heavier censure than outward profligacy or absolute neglect.[1]

In conclusion, it may safely be asserted that Mahomet had no true conception of the tremendous respon-

[1] Comp. Farrar, "Life of Christ," i. 374, regarding the Jews.

sibility he was taking upon himself in arrogating the title of God's inspired ambassador, and in claiming to be the successor of those who in ages past had been the heralds of His will. The Koran claims to be a continuation of the earlier messages of Heaven, and to supplement and develop the teaching of the Law and the Gospel. Assuming such to be the case, we may fairly look to it to afford us clearer views of the Divine will and attributes, of life and death, of the provision made for man's spiritual and temporal difficulties; and in it we should find the way made more plain for securing to all mankind their inherent rights of life, liberty, and social and political well-being. Instead of this, darkness and retrogression are engraved on every page of the "Preserved Book," God's universal fatherhood is ignored, and in place of the finished sacrifice, the sinner is bid to plunge into the dark future, trusting in his own righteousness; in his service of the All-merciful the fetters of a minute ritual are substituted for that worship which we are taught is to be in spirit and in truth. Light and darkness are not more opposed than the loving dictates of the Gospel and the vengeful spirit of the Koran, in which hatred and oppression take the place of love and forgiveness of injuries, and the denunciations of the prophet contrast with the voice of the Good Shepherd, which speaks of peace and good-will to all mankind.

INDEX.

R

B

C

D

N

O

P

T

X

Y

Z